THE PHOTOGRAPHS: This volume contains two of the war's most famous photographs: the Marines raising the American flag on Iwo Jima and the atomic mushroom cloud. It also includes a dramatic series of photographs of the way it was on the beaches of Normandy on D-Day; a memorable picture of three 14-year-old members of Hitler's "Air Guard"; a shocking photograph of the hell that was Belsen, and the photograph which may be the last ever taken of Hitler.

THE WORDS: In this volume are Cornelius Ryan's stirring description of D-Day, Stalin's words of praise for the Allied achievement in Normandy, and Ernie Pyle's rugged, first-hand account of the dogged, bloody infantry fighting in Northern France. Here also are a Marine combat correspondent's ~~account~~ of a howling, maniacal Banzai atta ~~~~ t's

a Japanese survi ~~~~ a.

Eyewitness
History
Of
World
War II

Vol. 4
Victory

TEXT: ABRAHAM ROTHBERG
PICTURES: PIERCE G. FREDERICKS
MICHAEL O'KEEFE
DESIGN: ANTHONY LaROTONDA

A GALLERY EDITION
BANTAM BOOKS / NEW YORK

contents

EYEWITNESS HISTORY OF
WORLD WAR II / Volume 4: VICTORY
Bantam Gallery Edition / Published October 1962.
All rights reserved. Copyright ©
1962 by Bantam Books, Inc.
Published simultaneously in the United States
and Canada. Bantam Books are published
by Bantam Books, Inc. Its
trade-mark, consisting of the words
"Bantam Books" and the portrayal
of a bantam, is registered in the United States
Patent Office and in other countries.
Marca Registrada. Printed
in the United States of America. Bantam Books,
Inc., 271 Madison Ave., New York 16, N. Y.

1.

2.

3.

D- Day

"Operation Overlord": The Invasion of France

For more than two years the Allies had been building up their forces to breach Hitler's Fortress Europa. Preparations had been massive and detailed. Two million soldiers waited in a Britain that was a vast arsenal and armed camp. The Strategic Air Forces pounded the rail and road networks of France and Belgium, smashed at the industry of Germany, and softened up the Nazi-held Continent for invasion. On Tuesday, June 6, 1944, the invasion across the English Channel began. Because of poor visibility, high winds and rough seas, D-Day had been postponed from June 5, but the next day a giant armada of almost 5000 ships was heading for a 60-mile-long invasion beachhead along the Normandy coast.

The top-secret choice of invasion site had been dictated by a number of key considerations. Because the Germans expected the invasion across the Dover Straits to the Pas de Calais, the shortest route into Germany through an area with the best ports, the Normandy coast, less heavily manned and fortified, where there would be some element of surprise, was chosen. The Norman invasion coast did have ports within striking distance of either flank—Le Havre on the left and Cherbourg on the right—which when captured would simplify supplying and reinforcing the invading Allied

General Eisenhower, Allied Supreme Commander, confers with British General Montgomery and Air Marshal Tedder, Allied chiefs of ground and air forces.

9

armies. It was also within fighter range of England so a continuous air umbrella could protect the beachheads.

The secret of time and place were hard to keep. Intelligence agents had supplied the Germans with both. Moreover, German Intelligence had known since January 1944 that the signals alerting the French Resistance would be broadcast by BBC and would be lines from Paul Verlaine's poem, Chanson d'Automne:

The long sobs of autumn's violins,

Wounding my heart with a monotonous languor,

When the second line was broadcast the invasion would begin within 48 hours. But the Germans did not put complete confidence in their Intelligence agents, though one of them was valet to the British Ambassador to Turkey. There had also been "leaks" in England when a high-ranking American officer talked too freely

The Normandy landings—Allied soldiers pour ashore on Omaha Beach in the

and when a "test tape" announcing the invasion was prematurely broadcast over the radio teletype only a few days before D-Day.

To meet the Allied invasion and defend 600 miles of coast from Holland to Spain, Field Marshal Gerd von Rundstedt had 60 divisions, 10 of them Panzers. These were divided into two groups, Army Group B under Rommel, including the 88th Corps in Holland, the 15th Army in the Pas de Calais and the 7th Army in Normandy, and Army Group G under General Jacob von Blaskowitz in the south of France. Disagreements between Rundstedt and Rommel played into Allied hands. Rundstedt believed he did not have enough troops to defend the coastline; he knew that many of his divisions were recruited from Nazi-subjugated nationalities and his opinion of the Atlantic Wall was that it had "no

face of mines, "Rommel's asparagus" (the angle-iron obstacles), and gunfire.

depth and little surface. It was sheer humbug." His plan was to keep his best divisions and the bulk of his armor in mobile reserve well back from the coast, and then hurl it against the Allies after they had landed.

Rommel, however, was convinced that the crucial attack would be the initial onslaught. "The war will be won or lost on the beaches," he insisted. ". . . the first twenty-four hours of the invasion will be decisive." Because he believed that overwhelming Allied air superiority would prevent moving troops and tanks from the strategic reserve to the coast, Rommel proposed to have the infantry and armor concentrated right smack up against the Atlantic wall. Hitler supported Rommel with his Directive No. 51, commanding that the Allies be swept back into the sea immediately. Rommel, from the time he came to the Western Front in November 1943, set about strengthening the Wall with pillboxes, bunkers, mine fields, barbed wire and fields of machine-gun, mortar, and artillery fire. He had the offshore waters heavily mined and studded with obstacles and barbed wire, and he flooded and set up obstacles on fields in the rear of the Wall as insurance against airborne landings.

Although Hitler had "an intuition" that the landings would come in Normandy, his generals were agreed it would be in the Pas de Calais. The Allies deliberately fostered and reinforced this belief by a campaign of deception which paid rich rewards. Dummy supply and landing-craft concentrations were set up across from the Pas de Calais, troops were deliberately staged there, and a stream of messages reinforced the impression of great activity. Most important, the Allied bombing campaign pounded the Pas de Calais more heavily than any other target area. The deception campaign was continued even after D-Day and not until July 24, six weeks after the landings, did Hitler and his generals become convinced that Normandy was not a diversionary thrust. They then released some of the 15th Army's forces there to fight in Normandy, but by then it was too late.

The first blows of the invasion were delivered by parachute and glider troops dropped into France not long after midnight on June 6. The British 6th Airborne Division was to secure the beachhead's left flank east of the Orne; the U. S. 82nd and 101st Airborne Divisions, the right flank in the areas of St. Mère Eglise and Carentan-Isigny. Their jobs were also to create havoc and confusion, disrupt enemy communications and attack German strongpoints overlooking the beaches. Though many were dropped off course and far from their targets, though gliders were shot down and had their bottoms ripped out by Rommel's obstacles, though men were killed in air collisions, drowned in swamps weighed down by their packs or shot down by Germans as they were caught helpless in their chutes on trees, they took their objectives with impressive speed and courage.

During the night 2000 Allied planes blasted German positions, installations, and communications, and in the early dawn a massive naval bombardment poured shells and rockets on the Germans defending the beaches. Neither planes nor U-boats could get to the invasion armada through its protective screen of warships and its guardian umbrella of planes, though mines did take a toll of ships.

H-hour was 6:30 and the assault troops stormed ashore on five beaches, from west to east called Utah, Omaha, Gold, Juno, and Sword, the Americans on the first two, British and Canadians on the others. In some

Scenes along the landing area: (top row, left to right)
German artillery fire bursts among the invaders; Americans
going ashore; British hit the beach. (In the second row)
Troops leaving the landing craft which has brought them
in close to the shore; some of the paratroopers who survived the drop; aid for the wounded. (At left) British
troops bringing German prisoners down to the beach. In
spite of the trouble the American airborne troops had as-
sembling after the night drop, landings at Utah Beach went
relatively smoothly. At Omaha Beach an unexpected German division inflicted bloody casualties in fierce resistance to the first waves of Allied combat troops. By the
end of D-Day, however, the Allies were dug in on high
ground behind the beach and clearly in France for keeps.

places the landings were unaccountably easy but on Omaha and Juno beaches the fighting was bitter and bloody. Cornelius Ryan gives a panoramic picture of how that day went:

From two miles out the assault troops began to see the living and the dead in the water. The dead floated gently, moving with the tide toward the beach, as though determined to join their fellow Americans. The living bobbed up and down in swells, savagely pleading for the help the assault boats could not tender. Sergeant Regis McCloskey, his ammunition boat safely under way, saw the screaming men in the water, yelling for help, begging us to stop—and we couldn't. Not for anything or anyone. Gritting his teeth, McCloskey looked away as his boat sped past, and then, seconds later, he vomited over the side. Captain Robert Cunningham and his men saw survivors struggling, too. Instinctively their Navy crew swung the boat toward the men in the water. A fast launch cut them off. Over its loud-speaker came the grim words, "You are not a rescue ship! Get on shore!"

It was H-Hour.

They came ashore on Omaha Beach, the slogging, unglamorous men that no one envied. No battle ensigns flew for them, no horns or bugles sounded. But they had history on their side. . . .

All along Omaha Beach the dropping of the ramps seemed to be a signal for renewed, more concentrated machine-gun fire. . . . The ramps came down and men stepped out into water three to six feet deep. They had but one object in mind—to get through the water, cross 200 yards of the obstacle-strewn sand, climb the gradually rising shingle and then take cover in the doubtful shelter of a sea wall. But, weighted down by their equipment, unable to run in the deep water and without cover of any kind, men were caught in crisscrossing machine-gun and small-arms fire.

Men fell all along the water's edge. Some were killed instantly, others called pitifully for medics as the incoming tide slowly engulfed them. . . .

Less than a third of the men survived the bloody walk from the boats to the edge of the beach. Their officers were killed, severely wounded or missing, and the men, weaponless and shocked, huddled at the base of the cliffs. . . .

Misfortune piled upon misfortune for the men of Omaha Beach. Soldiers now discovered that they had been landed in the wrong sectors. Some came in almost two miles away from their original landing areas. . . . Companies that had been trained to capture certain objectives never got near them. Small groups found themselves pinned down by German fire and isolated in unrecognizable terrain, often without officers or communications. . . .

Small islands of wounded men dotted the sand. Passing troops noticed that those who could sat bolt upright as though immune to any further hurt. They were quiet men, seemingly oblivious to the sights and sounds around them. . . .

Men lay shoulder to shoulder on the sands, stones and shale. They crouched down behind obstacles; they sheltered among the bodies of the dead. Pinned down by the enemy fire which they had expected to be neutralized, confused by their landings in the wrong sectors, bewildered by the absence of the sheltering craters they had expected from the air force bombing, and shocked by the devastation and death all around them, the men froze on the beaches. They seemed in the grip of a savage paralysis. Overwhelmed by it all, some men believed the day was lost. . . .

The shock would not last long. Even now a few men here and there, realizing that to stay on the beach meant certain death, were on their feet and moving.

Savagely, inch by inch, men fought their way off Bloody Omaha. . . .

Ranging up and down the 1st Division sector, oblivious to the artillery and machine-gun fire that raked the sands, was the 16th's commanding officer, Colonel George A. Taylor. "Two kinds of people are staying on this beach," he yelled, "the dead and those who are going to die. Now let's get the hell out of here."

As the men found it possible to move forward, their fear and frustration gave way to an overpowering anger. Near the top of the Vierville bluff, Ranger P.F.C. Carl Weast and his company commander, Captain George Whittington, spotted a machine-gun nest manned by three Germans. As Weast and the captain circled it cautiously, one of the Germans suddenly turned, saw the two Americans and yelled, "Bitte! Bitte! Bitte!" Whittington fired, killing all three. Turning to Weast, he said, "I wonder what bitte means."

Against the 7 infantry divisions, 1 Panzer division, and 2 Panzers in close reserve, the Allied landings threw 5 divisions in addition to the 3 airborne divisions dropped behind the lines. From the beginning, good luck and bad, good judgment and bad, swift action and delay on both sides played their parts.

But neither bad luck nor mistakes kept Allied courage and skill from storming and holding the beaches, and the degree of tactical surprise achieved and the curtain of fire Allied planes and warships laid down on German defenses kept over-all casualties relatively light. D-Day brought only some 11,000 casualties, about 2500 of those killed, far less than had been feared.

The build-up: Allied men, machines and supplies pour onto and off the beach.

A GI takes cover behind a hedgerow during house-to-house fighting. Norman

The critical factor was reinforcements. The pre-invasion Allied bombing had so badly wrecked road and rail networks that now, aided by good weather and sabotage by the French Resistance, Allied air superiority kept the Germans from getting through. Allied planes smashed German columns en route so that they arrived disorganized, decimated, and tired. These units were then thrown hastily into the battle piecemeal as they arrived. No concerted counterattack was mounted effective enough to throw the Allies into the sea.

On the other hand, the Allies were able to pour men and matériel ashore. Aware that even if French ports were captured quickly, Nazi demolitions would leave

houses, frequently built of stone, were fine forts and difficult to take.

them useless for weeks or months, the Allies had pre-fabricated two ports the size of Dover and towed them across the Channel, one for the Americans at Saint-Laurent-sur-Mer and the other for the British at Arromanches. These artificial harbors called "Mulberries" were a decisive factor in the invasion's success. In addition, Allied engineers made five breakwaters of scuttled blockships called "Gooseberries" and between Mulberries and Gooseberries a torrent of men and supplies were landed. Within five days the Allies had 16 divisions ashore; within a month more than 1,000,000 troops were in Normandy with 500,000 tons of supplies and 170,000 vehicles. Though the worst June storm in

British troops take cover behind a tank destroyer as Nazi snipers fire.

40 years hit the Normandy coast, sinking shipping, destroying the U. S. Mulberry and damaging the British one, this only held matters up slightly. The Arromanches Mulberry was repaired and continued to keep Allied soldiers reinforced and supplied.

Even the usually carping Stalin was forced to admire the achievement. "I cannot but admit," he wrote, "that the history of warfare knows no other like undertaking from the point of view of its scale, its vast conception, and its masterly execution. . . . History will record this deed as an achievement of the highest order."

In six days the separate Allied beachheads were joined into an 80-mile bridgehead, in some places 20 miles deep. One American spearhead sliced across the base of the Cotentin Peninsula and by June 17 had reached its west coast at Barneville and sealed the Peninsula off. Two other spearheads lunged north toward Cherbourg and stormed the port city on June 26 and 27, taking 35,000 prisoners, but were unable to prevent the Nazis from demolishing the harbor facilities.

Once having consolidated their bridgehead, the Allies tried to break out of it. Montgomery's plan was for a British thrust on the left flank around Caen, engaging the bulk of German armor, while the Americans burst out on the right flank. But the bocage country of Normandy was miserable terrain to fight in and Allied advantages in airpower and armor were minimized. The battle became a dogged, slogging fight that Ernie Pyle saw and described:

I want to describe to you what the weird hedgerow fighting in northwestern France was like. This type of fighting was always in small groups, so let's take as an example one company of men. Let's say they were working forward on both sides of a country lane, and the company was responsible for clearing the two fields

23

on either side of the road as it advanced. That meant there was only about one platoon to a field, and with the company's understrength from casualties, there might be no more than 25 or 30 men.

The fields were usually not more than 50 yards across and a couple of hundred yards long. They might have grain in them, or apple trees, but mostly they were just pastures of green grass, full of beautiful cows. The fields were surrounded on all sides by the immense hedgerows—ancient earthen banks, waist high, all matted with roots and out of which grew weeds, bushes, and trees up to 20 feet high. The Germans used these barriers well. They put snipers in the trees. They dug deep trenches behind the hedgerows and covered them with timber, so that it was almost impossible for artillery to get at them. Sometimes they propped up machine guns with strings attached so that they could fire over the hedge without getting out of their holes. They even cut out a section of the hedgerow and hid a big gun or tank in it, covering it with brush. Also they tunneled under the hedgerows from the back and made the opening on the for-

(Left) American troops under enemy fire advance through hedgerow barriers. (Below) A Nazi anti-tank gunner lies next to his gun. In the background are burned-out Nazi tanks.

ward side just large enough to stick a machine gun through. But mostly the hedgerow pattern was this: a heavy machine gun hidden at each end of the field and infantrymen hidden all along the hedgerow with rifles and machine pistols.

We had to dig them out. It was a slow and cautious business, and there was nothing dashing about it. Our men didn't go across the open fields in dramatic charges such as you see in the movies. They did at first, but they learned better. They went in tiny groups, a squad or less, moving yards apart and sticking close to the hedgerows on either end of the field. They crept a few yards, squatted, waited, then crept again.

If you could have been right up there between the Germans and the Americans you wouldn't have seen many men at any one time—just a few here and there, always trying to keep hidden. But you would have heard an awful lot of noise. Our men were taught in

Two GI's sleeping in a foxhole near the front line. Note the feet near the soldier's head. (Right) A French town left a shambles by the fighting as Americans pushed ahead.

training not to fire until they saw something to fire at. But the principle didn't work in that country, because there was very little to see. So the alternative was to keep shooting constantly at the hedgerows. That pinned the Germans to their holes while we sneaked up on them. The attacking squads sneaked up the sides of the hedgerows while the rest of the platoon stayed back in their own hedgerow and kept the forward hedge saturated with bullets. They shot rifle grenades too, and a mortar squad a little farther back kept lobbing mortar shells over onto the Germans. The little advance groups worked their way up to the far ends of the hedgerows at the corners of the field. They first tried to knock out the machine guns at each corner. They did this with hand grenades, rifle grenades and machine guns. . . .

The "Vengeance Weapons"

Hitler had ordered Rundstedt to sweep the Allied invasion into the sea by midnight of D-Day. That having failed, he ordered the Wehrmacht not to retreat a foot. The Führer announced that he had new, terrible weapons which would win the war, and these Vergeltungswaffe, retaliation or vengeance weapons, would pay the Allies back for their round-the-clock bombing of Reich cities.

Since 1943 Allied agents and aerial photographic reconnaissance had kept Allied Intelligence informed on flying bombs. They were developed at an experimental station on Peenemünde, an island in the Baltic Sea, and strange concrete launching platforms had been built for them along the coasts opposite England. Both Peenemünde and the launching sites were treated to continued heavy doses of Allied bombing, but on

June 13, a week after the D-Day landings, the first flying bomb hit London.

It was what the Germans called the V-1, and what Londoners eventually dubbed the "buzz bomb" or "doodlebug." The V-1 was an unmanned jet plane with a 1-ton explosive warhead. It flew about 3000 feet high at speeds up to 400 miles an hour and had a 250-mile range. Steered by magnetic compass it was easily able to hit large target areas, like London. During the three months of the summer of 1944, the Germans launched an average of 100 "buzz bombs" daily at England, a total of about 8000, but only a third, 2400, pierced the protective belts of fighter planes, anti-aircraft guns and barrage balloons. Even so the V-1s killed 6184 people and injured 17,981, and caused considerable damage to the city, but they did not undermine British civilian morale.

In early September the Nazis launched their V-2, a supersonic rocket also carrying a 1-ton explosive warhead, which shot up 50 miles high and hurtled down on Britain at a speed of 4000 miles an hour. The V-1 could be seen and heard and some defense evolved against it; the V-2 could neither be seen nor heard and there was no defense except capturing the launching ramps. In the 7 months before Allied armies overran the rocket sites in Holland, the Germans fired 1300 V-2s and about 500 hit London, killing 2724 people and injuring 6467. Altogether, the V-weapons inflicted some 35,000 casualties on the British and later, after the Allies had liberated Belgium, the Nazis turned the V-2s on Brussels and Liége and added more dead and injured to their score.

For some reason Hitler did not send the V-1s against either invasion staging areas at Portsmouth and Southampton, or at the beaches themselves, where they

To turn the tide, Hitler used his "vengeance weapons," the Flying V-1 and V-2 bombs. They renewed the devastation of the Blitz in London until the Allied armies surging forward were able to capture their Channel-coast launching sites.

might have caused considerable damage and perhaps even impeded the invasion. Nor did he succeed in destroying Londoners' morale for, as Churchill said, the "retribution" weapons were defeated by "the fortitude of the people who, by their conduct for the second time in this war, gave 'Greater London' a prouder meaning." And though Hitler had pinned great hopes

31

Duce and Führer inspect damages to the building where the July 20th plot on Hitler's life took place and failed.

on the V-weapons, they came too late to exert a decisive influence on the war's outcome.

The July 20th Plot

There were those in Germany who had retribution weapons for Hitler himself. These anti-Nazis came from many levels of German society—former government officials, civil servants, Social Democrats, intellectuals, church leaders. Their views ranged the political spectrum from conservative to radical and they opposed Hitler for a variety of reasons, some idealistic and patriotic, some shabby and opportunistic. But the most important group in the opposition came from among the Wehrmacht officer corps and the General Staff. Since the earliest days of Nazism, some Army officers, once they were aware that the Army had become Hitler's tool and not the reverse, had gone along with the Führer only as long as he was successful. Now, these men saw their beloved Wehrmacht and Vaterland bled white and on the brink of disaster, and they finally became the moving force in a plot to assassinate Hitler. By removing him and the other top Nazis, they hoped to bring the war to an end and negotiate more lenient terms from the Allies before all was lost.

The leaders of the plot were General Ludwig Beck, former chief of the General Staff, and Karl Goerdeler, former Lord Mayor of Leipzig. The man chosen to kill Hitler was a young officer, Colonel Claus von Stauffenberg, descendant of one of Germany's eminent military families, a man who had lost an arm, all but two fingers, and an eye in Africa, and one of the few men who in the normal course of his duties had access to Hitler. Twice before, von Stauffenberg had failed to go through with the assassination because Göring and Himmler were absent, and the plotters wanted to kill all three together.

But at a conference on July 20, 1944, at Hitler's Wolfschanze—or Wolf's Lair—headquarters near Rastenburg in East Prussia, Stauffenberg made a third attempt. He placed a briefcase containing a bomb at Hitler's feet and left the room. Another officer, finding the briefcase in his way, moved it behind one of the conference table's heavy legs. When the bomb exploded, therefore, the table leg and the heavy oaken table top, and the fact that the meeting was taking place in a wooden barracks because of warm weather, minimized the blast effect and saved Hitler's life.

Though four of the officers present were killed and twenty others wounded, Hitler escaped with only minor injuries. But he never recovered from the physical and emotional shock. His megalomania grew and he looked on himself as providentially preserved to be savior of the Reich. His self-pity swelled too and he thought the Reich no longer deserved him.

Hitler moved swiftly to crush the conspiracy. He instituted a purge so drastic and brutal that it put even the Röhm purge in the shade. Estimates are that more than 4500 people were executed, and as Allen Dulles commented, "Thousands were rounded up, arrested, tortured and killed in order that Hitler's Thousand-Year Reich might survive another 290 days."

The Battle of France

Two weeks after D-Day, Hitler held a conference with Rundstedt and Rommel at Margival, near Soissons, and both Field Marshals advised withdrawing the 7th Army to the Seine where, with the 15th Army, and given some room for mobile maneuver, they could fight more effectively. Hitler refused to permit them to surrender a foot of Norman ground. When a V-1 accidentally went off course and exploded close to the conference, Hitler quickly returned to Berchtesgaden instead of inspecting the troops and the front lines. At a second conference Hitler promised them new weapons to revolutionize the military situation, but his orders were still to stand fast in Normandy. When Field Marshal Wilhelm Keitel asked Rundstedt what to do, Rundstedt acidly answered: "Make peace, you idiots! What else can you do?" The following day he was relieved and on July 3 replaced by Field Marshal Günther von Kluge.

On July 17, a strafing Allied fighter raked Rommel's

car on a road near Caen and put Rommel out of the war with a skull fracture. Now, both senior German commanders in Normandy were out of the battle, and Kluge had both of their jobs. Rommel was later implicated in the July 20th assassination plot by some of his fellow officers. In October, having almost completed his convalescence, the "Desert Fox" was given the choice of being tried by a People's Court or taking poison so that Hitler would take no reprisals against either his family or staff, and after he did, Hitler gave out that the "Desert Fox" had died of his wounds.

Meantime, American troops were quickly shifted south from Cherbourg and once more began to try to break out of their bridgehead. The pivots of the German defense line were Caen, facing the British, and Saint-Lô, facing the Americans, and during July savage battles were fought for both. Beyond Caen stretched good open tank country, and Rouen and Paris. Also, a breakthrough there would split the German 7th Army south of the Seine from the 15th Army north of it. Consequently, the Germans concentrated most of their armor around Caen. The Americans fought a slogging infantry battle through the hedgerows to take Saint-Lô, suffering more than 10,000 casualties in 12 days. But when an enterprising American, Sergeant Curtis Colin, came up with a hedge-cutting device, the bocage stalemate was broken. By putting two steel blades on the front of a Sherman tank it was able to cut through the hedgerows. Ironically, the steel shears used were made of the tetrahedon angle-iron obstacles Rommel had strewn over the Normandy beaches. Paced by these "Rhinoceros" tanks, the Americans smashed into Saint-Lô on July 25 while the British, in fierce fighting, finally took Caen, cleared the heights around it, and seized the road network out of it on the 19th.

(Above) American howitzers clear the way to St. Lô, the pivot of the German defenses in Normandy. (Right) Infantry in St. Lô hit the dirt in the face of German small-arms fire. (Below) Americans, strung out, move up past a knocked-out Tiger tank. Once the St. Lô salient fell, Allied troops broke into the open plains of central France and plunged toward Paris.

To break the Caen and Saint-Lô deadlocks, heavy bombers were used in close support of the ground troops for the first time. Their bombs leveled both towns, leaving rubble blocking the progress of Allied tanks, and many of their bombs fell short on Allied troops in the front lines, inflicting heavy casualties. Among the victims was Lieutenant-General Lesley J. McNair, chief of the U. S. Army Ground Forces, who was observing the fighting in forward positions.

With fighter planes scouting before them, General George S. Patton's Third Army columns of tanks, armored cars, mobile guns and motorized infantry raced through Avranches at the end of July into Brittany and the plains of central France. A week later they had dashed 100 miles south through Rennes to Nantes on the Loire River and cut off the Breton Peninsula. Aided by the French Resistance, other Third

British tanks roll past a supply truck column during the Normandy breakout.

Army spearheads had rocketed to the end of the Peninsula in five days and bottled the Germans up in the large ports: Lorient, Saint-Nazaire, and Brest. Though these ports were now neutralized as U-boat bases, they were still denied to the Allies as supply ports. Instead of trying to storm them, General Omar N. Bradley had only light covering forces left to keep the Nazis there besieged and turned Patton east.

The Third Army wheeled and struck east through Laval toward the vital railroad center of Le Mans. With General Courtney H. Hodges' First Army pushing toward Vire and Mortain, and Lieutenant General Miles Dempsey's British Second Army and Lieutenant General H. D. Crerar's First Canadian Army pushing southeast from Caen toward Falaise, the Germans were threatened with envelopment. At Hitler's orders, instead of retreating to the Seine as he wished to do, Kluge counter-

Troops close in on a farmhouse after big guns have smashed it and set it afire.

Allied planes strafing and bombing German supply columns played a crucial role in the Normandy victory. (Left) Nazi trucks go up in smoke after strafing. (Below) A P-47 Thunderbolt pulls out after blowing up an enemy transport. (Above) The flamboyant tank commander, General George Patton (center), affecting the pearl-handled revolvers he so liked.

attacked on August 7, throwing 6 Panzer divisions at the narrow Avranches corridor. If he could crash through to the sea, his crumbling left flank might be saved and Patton's Third Army echelons cut off. After four days of stubborn First Army resistance, backed by massive Allied artillery shelling, fighter-bomber attacks on Nazi transport and communications, and brilliant tank-busting by rocket-firing Typhoons and Thunderbolts, the Panzer spearheads were blunted far short of their target.

While Kluge counterattacked, Patton's Third Army columns captured Le Mans, then turned north through Alencon toward Argentan, simultaneously striking Kluge's left flank and threatening to cut him off. The other half of the pincers, the British and Canadians, drove southeast from Caen, and between them they penned the 7th Army into a triangular salient. The apex was at Mortain and the open base was between Falaise and Argentan, the only German escape route. Kluge tried desperately to save his troops before they were completely surrounded, but between August 16 and 21, the Allies slammed the trap shut. Though more than a third of the 7th Army managed to escape, it had to leave most of its heavy guns, tanks, and vehicles behind. The retreat now turned into a rout and disorganized German units fled across the Seine. Altogether the battles of Normandy and France had been a German debacle. Since D-Day the Germans had suffered 240,000 troops killed and 210,000 prisoners.

While the Germans in the Falaise pocket were being annihilated, Patton's Third Army columns had driven ahead to take Orléans and Chartres, and sent spearheads to the Seine, cutting Paris off at Mantes on the northwest and at Melun on the southeast. Allied strategy was to avoid a battle for Paris and concen-

trate on destroying the remaining German troops in the field, but the Paris FFI (French Forces of the Interior) took matters into their own hands. Though Kluge had declared Paris an open city, they organized a revolt to free it on August 19. The Germans retaliated and General Eisenhower swiftly dispatched the French 2nd Armored Division under General Jacques LeClerc and the U. S. 4th Division to their aid. By August 25 Paris was liberated. After four years of Nazi occupation, Parisians greeted the Allied soldiers with joy, tears, flowers, fireworks, champagne, and kisses. The next day General de Gaulle arrived to install his Provisional French Government.

As the Allies approached Paris, 50,000 Frenchmen organized an attack on the Germans. The battle raged for six days.

The Liberation of Paris: Civilians take cover in the Place de la Concorde when small groups of Germans who still remained in the city opened fire. (Below) One of General Le Clerc's French troopers arrives in Paris and is welcomed home.

Invasion of Southern France

Once it was clear that the Allies would be victorious in Normandy, Churchill tried to persuade Roosevelt and Generals Marshall and Eisenhower to cancel the invasion of southern France called "Anvil." With the end of the war in view, Churchill pointed out that the im-

45

portant thing was the shape of political things to come. He plumped for a thrust across the Adriatic Sea to the Istrian Peninsula, up into Austria and Hungary, and southeast into Yugoslavia. Churchill emphasized that Britain had in part fought the war to prevent Nazi hegemony over Central Europe and it was not eager to exchange it for Soviet hegemony there.

Roosevelt, on the other hand, was worried about maintaining good relations with Stalin who, at the Teheran Conference, had opposed any landing in southeast Europe. Moreover, 1944 was the year of an American presidential election and if the Allies were stopped in Normandy it might mean losing the November political sweepstakes. Further, Eisenhower insisted that divisions were piling up in U. S. ports which could not be brought into play because he had no ports in France at which to debark them.

The Americans prevailed, and on August 15, the Seventh Army under General Alexander M. Patch landed on a 15-mile beachhead southwest of Cannes. Almost 50,000 of General Pierre Koenig's French Maquis helped make the campaign go even more smoothly and swiftly. Though General Blaskowitz had 10 divisions to oppose Patch's 3 U. S. divisions and General Jean de Lattre de Tassigny's 7 French ones, he put up little resistance and inflicted very few casualties, and the Seventh Army drove up the Rhone Valley. Within two weeks Marseilles and Toulon were captured, and on September 3, the Allies were in Lyons, on the fifth in Besançon, on the seventh in Dijon, and on the eleventh joined with Patton's Third Army right flank at Sombernon, between Dijon and Belfort. Blaskowitz managed to keep his forces from being cut off, though the French and Americans took 80,000 prisoners, and except for the Bay of Biscay ports, freed southern France.

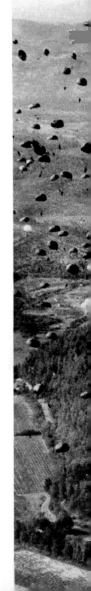

Allied landings in southern France were aided by a dummy airborne drop.

To the German Border

Paris was only a pause in the Allied advance. By mid-September Patch and LeClerc were in the Mulhouse-Belfort Gap; Patton's Third Army, plunging for the Saar Basin, was on the Moselle River on a broad front and had crossed it between Metz and Nancy; Hodges' First Army had fanned through the Ardennes, liberated Luxembourg, pierced the Siegfried line at two points and was threatening the German cities of Aachen and Trier. The British breakout on the left flank was as brilliant a blitzkrieg as Patton's had been on the right flank at Avranches. British and Imperial tanks and armored columns smashed into open country from the Caen hinge and lunged ahead 250 miles in six days. Racing forward at 40 miles a day, they broke across the Seine, took Rouen on August 30, Amiens the next day, Dieppe on September 1 (the Canadians avenging the Dieppe debacle of August 1942), took Brussels on the third and were in Antwerp on the fourth. So swift was their advance that the Nazis were unable to demolish the port facilities.

In a little more than three months from D-Day, the Allies had advanced to a continuous front from Ostend on the Channel coast to the Swiss border, and had the second largest port in Europe with its harbor facilities intact, though the Germans still controlled access to the port from the sea along the Scheldt Estuary.

Following the Falaise defeat Hitler replaced Kluge with Field Marshal Walter Model. After writing Hitler that he had to end the hopeless battle in the West, Kluge took poison and died. Though Hitler now permitted Model to withdraw to the Siegfried line—he had little choice—within three weeks he had replaced him with Rundstedt, calling the older general back to command for the third time. Rundstedt moved swiftly to piece the Wehrmacht's shattered divisions together into a coherent fighting force as they straggled back from France, and to establish a new line running along the Dutch border, the German frontier from Aachen to Trier, along the Moselle River and down through the Vosges Mountains. Then Rundstedt tried to reinforce his formations with new divisions wrested from the Luftwaffe and Navy, and with new levies of home guard soldiers called Volksgrenadier divisions. At the same time, he hurried to strengthen the Siegfried line which Hitler had weakened to bolster the Atlantic wall.

Germany was now being pressed on all sides, and was in dire straits. Between June and September the Reich had lost 2,000,000 troops killed or taken prisoner; on the Western Front alone, 350,000 Germans had been taken prisoner, and 240,000 killed and wounded. Against this the Allies had sustained 235,000 killed, wounded and captured. In addition, another 200,000 Nazi troops were besieged in the Channel and Atlantic ports. Moreover, the Germans had lost vast amounts of equipment in France, and on the Russian front, and Allied air strikes had so badly damaged their synthetic oil industry that they could neither put all their armor into the field nor all their planes into the air.

The Germans in the Atlantic and Channel ports denied them to the Allies so most supplies had to come across the beaches, through the British Mulberry at Arromanches, or through Cherbourg. Allied bombings had so devastated the French railway network that supplies had to be carried the 400 miles from the beach to the forward columns by truck. With 2,000,000 troops now in France and 36 divisions in action, each of them requiring 600-700 tons of supplies a day,

The airborne invasion of Holland called for an Anglo-American
Army to seize strategic bridges and hold them while infantry
rushed to their support, thereby outflanking the Siegfried
line. But in spite of a gallant fight by the paratroops, the
Nazis cut them to ribbons. After nine days, the British
1st Airborne was ordered to retreat. Only a third got back.

As autumn set in, roads turned bad and the trucks which had supplied the swift

some 20,000 tons of supplies a day had to be moved from the beaches to the spearheads. Most important, Allied armor needed gasoline. Though Allied ingenuity strove to meet the demand with the underwater fuel pipeline from Britain to the Continent, with the Red Ball Express trucks which hauled gasoline from the coast to the front along a one-way, round-the-clock, high-speed highway, and with air transport from Britain, supply lines were so overextended and heavily taxed that the Allied armies ground to a halt just short of the German border.

At that point, while the weather was still good, Montgomery called for a major thrust of 40 Allied divisions under his single command to smash across the lower Rhine, outflank the Siegfried line, and dash into the north German plain. To do so meant concentrating all Allied supply and maintenance resources behind that single effort, and halting all other Allied armies. There was also the alternative possibility of massing 40 divisions under General Patton, giving him

advance bogged down. The infantry fought on, bundled against the bitter cold.

priority of supply, and sending him hurtling through the Saar to cut Germany in two across the country's narrow waist. Montgomery preferred the northern thrust because armor could more easily be deployed on the north German plain, because his left flank would be protected by the sea, because the remaining V-1 and V-2 launching sites could be overrun, but most important because Berlin and the Ruhr were more important politically and industrially than any targets available to Patton.

It was a brilliant and daring scheme, but Eisenhower was not sure it could be supplied and maintained, nor was he certain that the Germans were as close to collapse as Montgomery believed. Moreover, Eisenhower was under great pressure from Generals Bradley and Patton to continue their advance on the right wing. For Montgomery's plan to succeed, Eisenhower had to transfer General Hodges' First Army to his command and part of the SHAEF (Supreme Headquarters Allied Expeditionary Forces) agreements was for American armies to be under American commanders. Eisenhower, therefore, decided to compromise. Instead of Montgomery's "narrow" thrust, he ordered the more certain "broad front" movement to the German border, and gave Montgomery and Patton parity of supplies. At the same time, however, he gave Montgomery the go-ahead for the first step in a riskier concentrated "narrow" thrust: an airborne operation across the lower Rhine at Arnhem.

On September 17, Montgomery launched "Operation Market-Garden," a bold airborne invasion of Holland intended to outflank the Siegfried line above its northern German plain. Simultaneously, the assault would split Holland in two cutting off the V-2 sites and 350,000 German troops in western Holland. The British 1st Airborne, the U. S. 82nd and 101st Airborne Divisions were dropped from north to south to seize strategic bridges — at Arnhem over the lower Rhine, at Nijmegen over the Waal, and at Grave over the Maas — and to force and hold open a corridor from the Dutch border to Nijmegen. The British Second Army, from its footholds on the north bank of the Meuse-Escaut Canal, sent 3 crack divisions racing north up that corridor to join the airborne troops. Arnhem was 70 miles away and the plan was to relieve the "Red Devils" of the 1st Airborne there in three days.

From the beginning things went wrong. Instead of the airborne force concentrating against the Germans in a single stroke, the air drop took three days because there weren't enough planes to do the whole job at once. By then bad weather set in and made it difficult to reinforce and supply the troops by air. The Germans captured the Allied battle plan in one of the first gliders they shot down and, knowing Allied strength and intentions, were able to concentrate their counterattacks quickly and in the right places. Moreover, Allied Intelligence had not known that the battletried 2nd SS Panzer Corps was refitting in the Arnhem area, and it was quickly thrown into the fighting. To make matters still worse, the "Red Devils" were dropped too far from the Arnhem Bridge and couldn't get to it.

Though all the other bridges were seized by U. S. airborne and British ground forces aided by members of the Dutch Resistance, and the narrow corridor to Nijmegen secured, it was constantly attacked from the flanks and cut, so that the ground forces could not advance quickly enough to relieve the "Red Devils." While the ground forces were stalled, the Germans sealed the paratroopers off into a pocket 9 miles by 5 and cut them to ribbons. Allied efforts to drop the beleaguered airborne troops reinforcements, food, and ammunition proved almost fruitless, and British ground forces could make no further headway against fierce Nazi resistance than the south bank of the Rhine across from Arnhem. Only a few miles, but a critical distance. After nine days and nights of continuous fighting, Montgomery ordered the 1st Airborne to retreat. On the night of September 25, about 2400 of the original 10,000 made their way across the river to Allied lines.

Having failed to flank the Siegfried line, the Allies now turned to solving their supply problems by clearing the ports in their wake. During September the Canadian First Army secured the Channel ports, taking Le Havre, Boulogne and Calais, while the U. S. Ninth Army under the command of General William H. Simpson captured Brest and 37,000 prisoners on September 20, after 6 weeks of fierce assault. The major objective was Antwerp, where German control of the approaches to the city continued to deny the port to the Allies. Driving the Germans out of Breskens, South Beveland, and Walcheren Island was a bitter, bloody battle. Supported by naval gunfire, by RAF bombers smashing the Westkapelle dike to flood Walcheren's defenses, and by air bombing and strafing, the Canadians and Royal Marine Commandos cleared the coastlines commanding the Scheldt Estuary in a slogging combination of amphibious assault and infan-

try fighting. It took until November 9 and though the Canadians captured 12,500 prisoners, they suffered 27,633 casualties, a very heavy price. After Allied minesweepers cleared the 70 miles of heavily mined Estuary, the first convoys began to unload at Antwerp on November 28.

With ports available, the Allies during the autumn, built up their supply depots, reinforced their troops, repaired France's roads, railways, and bridges, and,

Infantrymen with rifle grenades cleaning out a house in Belgium held by Nazis.

With artillery clearing the ground ahead and tanks to spearhead the attack, the Allies broke through the vaunted Siegfried line and were on the Rhine at several points. Then winter came, slowing the infantry and bringing overcast days which grounded the British and American tactical air power.

after the fall of Brest, brought the U. S. Ninth Army into the line. There were now 7 Allied armies facing the Germans from the sea to the Swiss border: the First Canadian, Second British, Ninth, First, Third, and Seventh American, and the First French, in that order. All but the Canadians pressed forward against the two major Allied objectives: the Ruhr and Saar Basins. Winter, rain, and mud slowed the advance, and the Germans, now fighting on their own soil, resisted stubbornly, but the Allies moved ahead. In October, after three weeks of bloody fighting, Hodges' First Army pierced the Siegfried line and took the first major German city, Aachen. Then, all during November, in as bitter a battle as the Allies had encountered, Hodges' troops fought through the Hurtgen Forest toward the Roer River, last obstacle before the Rhine. North of them, the British Second and the U. S. Ninth also pushed toward the Roer. In November, Patton's Third Army captured Metz, though some of its fortresses held out for another month, then closed up on the Saar border and threw three bridgeheads across the Saar River. By mid-December Patch's Seventh Army had captured Strasbourg, and with the French First was on the Rhine in a solid front except where the Germans retained a small salient on the river's west bank, the Colmar pocket.

Battle of the Bulge

While the Allies consolidated their positions, refitting and redeploying their troops, the Germans had time to recover. The fanatical defense of the port garrisons had earned them breathing space in which to strengthen their own dispositions and defenses. More than that, since September Hitler had planned a counterattack and secretly gathered a formidable force opposite the Ardennes to carry it out. Three rested, reorganized and re-equipped armies were massed there under over-all command of Rundstedt. There were 250,000 men in more than 30 divisions, 11 of them Panzers, 14 or 15 motorized infantry, with 2000 tanks and 3000 planes, and large quantities of assault artillery.

Their task was to repeat Rundstedt's 1940 success against the French: they were to break through the Ardennes, cross the Meuse River, then turn north to strike for Antwerp. If they reached the sea, the Allied armies would be split in two, with four Allied armies trapped in Holland and Belgium with no way of retreating or escaping, and the entire Allied front would be shattered. To help the armor and infantry to race ahead, parachute troops, saboteurs, and English-speaking troops in American uniforms and vehicles were to strike at key points, play havoc in the American rear, and seize the bridges over the Meuse.

In the offensive against the Ruhr and the Saar, the Allies had been forced to thin the center of their lines, facing the Ardennes Forest, so that a single corps, Major General Troy H. Middleton's VIII Corps, held almost 90 miles of front. Four divisions, two recovering from the Hurtgen Forest bloodbath, one green division being battle tested, and one armored division, held the entire line. Against these, in the early morning fog of December 16, Rundstedt threw three armies in a powerful thrust concentrated on a 50-mile front between Monschau and Echternach. Tactical surprise was complete and the overwhelming German power broke through the American lines and fanned out toward the Meuse. But this was not 1940, these troops were not the demoralized French Army,

Against the thinly held Allied front in the Ardennes, Hitler desperately

launched a last counterattack with three armies and 250,000 combat troops.

Captured German pictures show the offensive in the Bulge surging ahead. However, a green American infantry division held the northern shoulder of the Nazi salient, the 7th Armored Division died at St. Vith to delay the assault for six days, and the 101st Airborne stood fast at Bastogne.

nor were the Germans the old Wehrmacht. Some American units broke and retreated, but others stood their ground and grimly fought back.

Bad weather grounded the Allied air forces and the land battle hinged chiefly on who could command the road junctions. Because the Ardennes is rugged terrain, heavily forested, mechanized forces are in the main confined to the roads and the road network itself is limited. The crucial junctions were Saint-Vith and Bastogne, the latter the hub of seven roads.

In desperate fighting, the U. S. 7th Armored Division held Saint-Vith for six days against a battering German assault, slowing the Nazi drive for the Meuse at a critical moment, until the Americans and Saint-Vith were overwhelmed on December 21. While remnants of the 28th Infantry Division and of the 9th and 10th Armored Divisions held the Germans off at Bastogne, Eisenhower sent the 101st Airborne Division racing to defend the town from Rheims where they were recuperating from the Arnhem jump. By December 20, they had dug in around Bastogne and were surrounded by Germans, about 18,000 Americans facing three German divisions of some 45,000 men. General S. L. A. Marshall gives an account of the fighting:

It was a night for drifters, the night of December 19-20. As the darkness grew, more men from the elements which had been shattered to the east of Bastogne came moving back through the regimental lines of the 101st. Few of them stayed. Colonel Ewell and his officers talked to these men. They could tell very little of what had happened to them. Many were inarticulate. Infantrymen from units of the 28th Division still trickled into the area in groups of three or four. They made no attempt to organize themselves and they did not for the most part wish to be organized by anyone else. Some of these straggling infantrymen would ask Ewell's men, "What are you doing?" Upon being told, "We are fighting Germans," they would look at the paratroopers as if they were stark mad.

But not all were like that. Some who seemed utterly wretched and spent when they came to within the lines, upon being handed a K ration, would eat it and look around and ask where they could get a rifle. They were ready to fight again. But to others food and companionship made no difference. They had been shocked so badly that they wanted only to keep drifting. They were allowed to do so. This disorder had no ill effect on the combat force. The demoralization did not seem to bother the nerves of the men who were still fighting and they accepted it as the natural product of battle it often is. . . .

That was the beginning. Almost nothing that followed could be seen as clearly. During the next two hours the defensive perimeter was under constant attack from the German armor and infantry. But the enemy pressure developed quite unevenly as if their forces, too, were groping or were keeping active simply to conceal some larger design. It was battle with the bewildering shifts of a montage; there were momentary exposures and quick shifting of scene. The enemy came on in groups of a few tanks supported by small parties of infantry and were held off by the armored infantry and paratroopers with their own weapons just long enough to let a friendly tank or tank destroyer get into firing position. Fog mixed with smoke from the burning buildings again mantled the country between the village and the ridges, diffusing the efforts of both forces. It was all but impossible for anyone to get any impression of how the tide was moving; the combatants could tell only what went

67

Weary soldiers of the 101st Airborne take a breather during the Bastogne siege.

on right before their eyes. . . .

The Germans concentrated on reducing that vital communications hub, but they failed. On December 22, they offered the "Battered Bastards of Bastogne" an "honorable surrender" and got Brigadier General Anthony C. McAuliffe's cryptic, "Nuts," in reply.

German spearheads pushed 65 miles through the American lines to within three miles of the Meuse east of Dinant, but here they were stopped. American reaction had been swift, violent and intelligent. German parachutists and saboteurs, were discovered, and killed or captured. The bridges over the Meuse remained in Allied hands, and the flanks of the 35-mile-wide "bulge" held. In a brilliant 7-day maneuver, Patton reversed the Third Army's front from eastward facing the Saar to northward facing the German salient, and then drove into the German left flank. Hodges' First and Simpson's Ninth Armies struck south into the Nazi right flank, to pinch off the salient. On December 22 the weather turned fair and Allied planes bombed and strafed the German front and rear unmercifully and without letup. By the day after Christmas, Patton's armor had driven a wedge through the encircling Germans to Bastogne. As his flanks were pressed inward and encirclement threatened, Rundstedt withdrew to the east in good order.

By the end of January the "Battle of the Bulge" was over and the Allied lines restored to where they had been before the German counterattack. The Nazis had sustained 90,000 casualties, with 13,000 dead. American casualties numbered about 77,000, with 8600 dead.

Hitler had squandered Germany's last precious reserves. With these expended, he had nothing left to stave off defeat in either the west or the east.

Victory in Europe

Red Army Triumphant

Four days after D-Day in Normandy, the Red Army launched the series of offensives which not only cleared the Nazis from Soviet soil, but knocked three of Germany's satellites out of the war before the year's end. Though most of the Nazi armed strength was deployed against them—200 German divisions of more than 1,500,000 men—the Red Armies had 300 divisions of some 4,500,000 men, a 3-1 superiority, and an overwhelming 5-1 superiority in tanks, guns and planes.

The first Russian onslaught was launched against the Finns on June 10. Though Finnish diplomatic negotiations for a separate peace had begun in Sweden in February 1944, nothing came of it, and now General Govorov's armies smashed through the Mannerheim line and captured Viipuri in 12 days.

In September, after replacing President Rysto Ryti, Marshal Mannerheim sued for peace. The armistice signed on September 16 gave the Russians all they had tried to take from Finland in 1940, in addition to the Petsamo district, and a 50-year lease on the Porkkala Peninsula, plus a $300,000,000 indemnity. Unwilling to relinquish their hold on Finland, the Germans retreated slowly, scorching the earth in their wake, but the Finns opposed this and war broke out between them. Not until October did the Russians clear 10 German divisions from the north of Finland, pushing them back across the Norwegian frontier and taking the Norwegian port of Kirkenes in the process.

All along the length of the front from the Baltic to the Black Sea, the Russians shifted the weight of their attack; as operations on one front were slowed, powerful offensives began on another. The Germans, continually off balance, never found enough breathing space to rebuild their lines.

On the Baltic front, the Red Army smashed around both sides of Lake Peipus and cleared Estonia of the Germans. They plunged through Latvia and Lithuania, isolating the remaining Germans in salients around Memel and in Courland, forced the Nieman River and pushed to the East Prussian border. In White Russia, Russian troops smashed the Fatherland line, hinged on the "hedgehog" fortresses of Vitebsk, Mogilev, and Bobruisk, and then encircled and captured Minsk, the main German base on the central front. In Poland, Russian forces took Bialystok, Brest-Litovsk, Lvov, and hurled the Germans back to the Vistula and the Carpathians. In the Lvov area, they forced the Vistula and established a powerful bridgehead, 47 miles long and 22 miles wide, on the western bank.

As victory over Germany came closer, so now the Soviet military advances highlighted the differences between Russia and its Western Allies, and clearly

A Nazi "superman" is herded to the rear by a Russian in the Red Army drive which lunged to the borders of the Reich.

As the Germans fell back, the Russians in the north knocked Finland out of the

demonstrated that the Russians' primary concern, even more than the military defeat of the Nazis, was to secure hegemony in Eastern and Central Europe.

The nub of these differences was most dramatically concerned with Poland. On August 1, when General Konstantin Rokossovski's Red Armies closed on Warsaw, General Tadeusz Bor-Komorowski's Polish Underground Home Army, which owed its loyalties to the Polish Government-in-Exile in London, and was also anti-Russian and anti-Communist, rose in revolt against the Nazis in the city. Moscow radio had called for the Poles to join the battle against the Germans "by direct active struggle in the streets, houses, etc., of

war and drove the battle-weary Nazis back toward the Fatherland's frontiers.

Warsaw" so that "the moment of final liberation will be hastened and the lives of our brothers saved." The Poles also hoped to establish some independence of the Soviets by contributing to their own liberation.

Just across the Vistula the Red Army columns now stopped. The Russians insisted this was due to supply and transport problems, and German counterattacks with newly reinforced divisions. The Red Army remained outside of Warsaw for two months while in a fierce house-to-house, street-to-street struggle, the Nazis crushed the 40,000-man Home Army, killed 15,000 of them, and deported large numbers to concentration camps.

It was obvious that the Russians were more than content to have the Nazis liquidate their political opponents and they refused to send relief to the embattled Poles. They disowned the Home Army as "adventurers," they said the revolt had not been coordinated with or approved by the Russian High Command, and that the insurrection was playing into German hands. When the Allied air forces dropped supplies from Italian bases 700 miles away, the Russians refused to let their planes land for refueling on the Russian bases near Warsaw; they insisted that the supplies were falling into German hands.

While the Red Armies halted on the vital central front between the Baltic Sea and the Carpathian Mountains — the shortest route to Germany — where Hitler had now concentrated the vast bulk of his armor, the Russians switched their offensive south to the front between the Carpathians and the Black Sea.

On August 20, two Russian armies under Generals Rodion Malinovsky and Fedor Tolbukhin jumped off from their bridgeheads across the Dniester River and tore the entire line apart. In two days they had captured Jassy and Kishinev, surrounded the German 6th Army and annihilated its divisions, and gone on to overrun Moldavia and Bessarabia. On the third day, August 23, King Michael, who since April had been putting out peace feelers to the Allies in Ankara, removed Marshal Ion Antonescu, replaced him with General Sanatescu, and had taken Romania out of the war. The next day the Luftwaffe bombed Bucharest in savage reprisal, and on the day following, Romania declared war on Germany and Hungary. Romanian divisions joined the Russians and not only caused the collapse of German resistance in the country, but permitted the Russians to take large numbers of

A swath of destruction and scorched earth was left in the Nazi Armies' wake.

prisoners, and to occupy the Ploesti oil fields, the Black Sea ports, and the Romanian rail system virtually intact so that Russian supply problems were greatly simplified. In the armistice signed in Moscow on September 12, the Romanians gave up to Russia the territory the Soviets had seized in 1940, promised to restore Allied properties and pay $300,000,000 indemnity within six years, and turn over its merchant marine. At the same time, the Romanians were accepted as co-belligerents and promised parts of Transylvania from Hungary.

Bulgaria had made peace overtures to the Allies in Turkey from July forward, but though the Bulgarians now swiftly pulled out of the war on August 26, avowing their neutrality, they refused to declare war on Germany and their troops continued to support the Germans in Greece and Yugoslavia. On September 5, the Russians declared war on Bulgaria and after four days the Bulgarians surrendered and Tolbukhin's columns occupied the country. A new Bulgarian government announced hostilities against Germany and on October 28 the armistice signed called for Bulgaria to give up territories seized in Greece and Yugoslavia.

With Romania and Bulgaria out of the war, and the Red Armies plunging up the Danube Valley, the Germans hurriedly began to evacuate their forces from Greece. Though harried by Greek and Yugoslav partisans, and flank attacks by their former Bulgarian allies, the Germans managed to extricate most of their troops, but abandoned garrisons on Crete and Rhodes.

On October 4, British troops landed at Patras, and encountering little German opposition, swept over the country in five weeks. But they had inherited a complex and bitter political heritage. During 1943 civil war broke out between the two main Greek resistance groups: the Communist-dominated E.A.M. ("National Liberation Front") and its armed forces E.L.A.S. ("People's National Army of Liberation") and the Republican and anti-Communist E.D.E.S. ("National Democratic Army"). Subsequently both factions fought more among themselves for postwar political power than they did against the Nazi invaders. Neither faction approved the British-supported Royal Greek Government-in-Exile, nor would either accept the return of King George II without a plebiscite. As Soviet armies swept into the Balkans and German evacuation of Greece became imminent, a mutiny in the Greek Army and Navy in Egypt broke out in April 1944 against the Royal Greek Government, and it was forcibly suppressed by British troops. An effort at compromise was then made to form a Greek government representing all contending groups under Social Democratic Premier M. Papandreou. But on December 3 a civil war broke out between E.L.A.S. and the Papandreou Government and Churchill ordered the British expeditionary force to intervene and crush the E.L.A.S. insurrection. A storm of protest swept Britain and the U. S. and widened the rift between the allies.

Churchill, always best in a tight spot, defended his stand vigorously. In the House of Commons, he sensibly pointed out that, "Democracy is not based on violence or terrorism, but on reason, on fair play, on freedom, on respecting the rights of other people. Democracy is no harlot to be picked up in the street by a man with a tommy gun." On Christmas Eve, 1944, while the Battle of the Bulge raged, he flew to Athens. There he succeeded in establishing a compromise but anti-Communist regency under Archbishop Damaskinos, with General Plastiras as Premier, got King George II to agree not to return to Greece

Its Balkan Allies gone, Germany was alone. (Above) Nazi gunners fight on.

"unless summoned by a free and fair expression of the national will," and so brought an uneasy peace to Greece.

Throughout the affair, Stalin abstained both from action and comment, but his absention, though assured by prior agreement, had been bought at a bitter price. In October 1944, on a visit to Moscow, Churchill had worked out a rough division of power in the Balkans with Stalin. The agreement assigned Russia 90 per cent predominance in Romania in exchange for 90 per cent dominance (with the U. S.) in Greece, Hungary and Yugoslavia were divided up 50-50, and in Bulgaria the Russians were accorded 75 per cent dominance. Stalin used this agreement and his absention from the Greek controversy to guarantee him a free hand in Romania and Bulgaria. Churchill insisted the agree-

ment was only temporary during military operations, and to be revised at the peace conference. Also, it did no more than recognize a fait accompli, because Soviet armies were already in control of the area, and Churchill said he wanted to save what he could.

While the alliance between Britain and the U. S. was showing signs of strain, Stalin's armies were well on their way to gaining control of southeastern Europe. Three Russian armies converged on Budapest. In October, General Petrov's troops drove south from Polish Galicia through the Carpathian passes into eastern Slovakia, too late to prevent Nazi suppression of a Slovak rising which left 20,000 Slovak dead in the mountains. Petrov's spearheads sliced into Hungary to outflank the Germans north of Budapest, forcing their withdrawal to the line of the Danube. At Miskolc, he joined Malinovsky's right wing and together, on December 3, they captured the city. From Bucharest, Malinovsky's army had raced up the Danube Valley, forced the Tisza River line at Szeged before the Germans could redeploy the troops they had evacuated from the Balkans to defend it, and penetrated the outskirts of Budapest in the second week of November. Here, met by stubborn Hungarian and German opposition, Malinovsky halted to wait for Tolbukhin's armies to come up. Tolbukhin had struck westward from Bulgaria into Yugoslavia and joined hands with Tito's Partisans to free Belgrade from the Nazis on October 20. Tolbukhin then wheeled, crossed the Danube, and hurtled northwest to join Malinovsky's left, and at the end of December completed the Red Army encirclement of Budapest.

The Hungarians had put out peace feelers to the Allies in March in Turkey, and Regent Admiral Miklós Horthy had asked for an armistice in mid-October. But the Nazis thwarted the plan and installed a new Hungarian Fascist Arrow Cross government under Premier Ferenc Szalasi. The Soviets consequently set up their own rival government which now declared war on Germany.

For the time being, the Russians were content also to leave their Yugoslav flank to be cleared by Marshal Tito. Tito, or Josip Broz, his given name, had been head of the Yugoslav Communist Party since 1937. He had lived in the USSR for a long time and been indoctrinated there.

After the Nazis invaded Yugoslavia in 1941, Draja Mihailovic, a colonel and former expert on guerrilla tactics in the Yugoslav Royal Army, had rallied a group of Serbs to continue guerrilla resistance to the enemy. They were called Chetniks. But Yugoslavia

Communist-trained Josip Broz—"Tito"—led a Yugoslavian resistance army.

was riven by rivalries between nationalist minorities—
Slovenes, Croats, Serbs—and by profound political
cleavages—republican, royalist, Communist, and Fascist, and soon a three-way civil war between Fascist
Ustachi, Chetniks, and Tito's Communist Partisans
raged. Tito's attempts to impose Communism on the
country, his mass execution of opponents, his exp o-
priation and burning of property, and his requisitioning
of supplies and grain, soon caused open civil conflict
between Chetniks and Partisans. Caught between the
civil war with Tito and savage German reprisals
Mihailovic sought an accommodation with the Axis.

With Mihailovic compromised, with no possibility
of agreement between Chetnik and Partisan, Churchill
supported Tito and disowned Mihailovic. Further, he
encouraged King Peter to dismiss the Chetnik leader,
who had been appointed Royal Minister of War, in the
hope that Tito's promises not to impose Communism
on Yugoslavia would be kept.

Yalta

There had been a series of conferences between the
Anglo-American leaders during the war, but Stalin
had been conspicuously and deliberately absent. He
had attended only one meeting outside of Russia, at
Teheran. By and large, the conferences had dealt
with military conduct of the war, with broad principles,
and Allied hopes and intentions. With the defeat of
Germany looming, it was urgent that the "Big Three"
make firm decisions on a whole spectrum of major
problems. All during fall 1944, Churchill had pushed
for such a conference, but both Roosevelt and Stalin
had delayed—Roosevelt because of the presidential
election and the inauguration; Stalin because he

wanted the Red Armies in a stronger position in East and Central Europe.

With the end of the war in Europe drawing near, opposition to Hitler and Nazi Germany no longer knit the three Great Powers together so closely; Yalta was planned to reconcile their differences. Roosevelt saw himself in the role of "mediator" between Britain and the Soviet Union, instead of recognizing the identity of Anglo-American interests, and it was this that as much as anything else caused the tragedy of Yalta.

The basic division was twofold: first, the British, long accustomed to the intricacies and realities of European power politics, constantly kept in mind that the war was a political instrument used for political ends. The Americans, partly out of naïveté and ignorance, partly out of idealism, insisted that military victory over the German Army was the prime objective and political settlements were something to be arrived at by the politicians after the war. The second division in some measure arose out of the first. Americans in general, and President Roosevelt in particular, though thoroughly anti-Communist, had little realistic appraisal of Soviet political methods and objectives. Idealistically concerned with reshaping a new, peaceful, and secure world without spheres of influence, balance of power or colonialism—concepts which Britain seemed the arch-exponent of—Americans did not comprehend the extent of Stalin's expansionist aims in Europe and Asia. American leaders thought they had to and could do business with Stalin, and they saw no clash of basic national interests.

To the Americans, British imperial ambitions and colonialism seemed a greater threat to a just and stable peace than did Soviet aggression. Britain was concerned to restore and bolster its security in West-

ern Europe, the Mediterranean, and in the Far East, as its political posture in Belgium, France, Greece, Italy, India, and Burma, among others, demonstrated. Churchill himself had informed Roosevelt: "Mr. President, I believe you are trying to do away with the British Empire." And after five years of war, and great losses in blood and treasure, Britain no doubt supported Churchill's public declaration: "We mean to hold our own. I have not become the King's First Minister in order to preside over the liquidation of the British Empire." Churchill's "percentage deal" with Stalin on the Balkans in October 1944 had inflamed American suspicions still further. De Gaulle, too, wanted France treated as a great power and its empire respected, and this was another Old World note of discord in the New World.

Underlying the national rivalries and conflicts of interest was a pervading sense that the Allies did not have a clear or unified policy for the peace. In the main, Allied policy, as seen in North Africa, Italy, France, Belgium, and Greece, seemed intent on avoiding the drastic social reform that the people of Europe seemed to expect, and on emphasizing orderly and stable governments organized on the foundation of the old social fabric.

The Soviet Union, on the other hand, had a very clear idea of what it wanted from the war. Stalin had always concentrated on the political shape of things to come. By the end of February 1945, the Red Army controlled every capital in Central and southeastern Europe except Prague and Athens, and, at Yalta, Stalin expected confirmation of his conquests and recognition of Soviet hegemony in these areas.

The major problems to be dealt with at Yalta concerned Germany, the war against Japan, the reorganization of Central and southeastern Europe, and the postwar United Nations organization which Roosevelt thought would guarantee a just and stable peace.

Agreement on what was least important to the Russians came easiest. A Declaration on Liberated Europe was jointly approved, affirming ideals the Great Powers had often espoused, promising to help those peoples liberated from Nazism and Fascism to establish internal peace, to relieve distressed peoples, and to "form interim governmental authorities broadly representative of all democratic elements in the population and pledged to the earliest possible establishment through free elections of governments responsive to the will of the people." But to accept this statement of principle and to implement it in reality were very different things.

The questions on Germany were profound and serious. Should the Reich be dismembered? What should the peace terms be? What would be done with war criminals? What reparations should Germany pay? What should the occupation zones be? What role should France play in the occupation?

Agreement was hammered out on unconditional surrender, on refusal to deal with war criminals, and on not partitioning Germany. Occupation zones were finally agreed to by the Big Three with joint Allied occupation of Berlin, but the Western Allies neglected to have their transit rights to Berlin clearly defined and guaranteed. The U. S. was not seriously put out by Stalin's refusal to let the French share in the occupation, but Britain was. Forewarned of American intentions to withdraw its armies from Europe within two years, Churchill wanted a powerful France to help occupy Germany and to reinforce Western European power against rising Soviet might. Stalin finally consented to let the French have a separate zone provided it was carved out of the British and American zones.

Stalin also was determined to dismantle 80 per cent of Germany's heavy industry and to extract $20,000,000,000 of reparations in kind, half to go to the Soviet Union. Though disinclined to rebuild a powerful Reich, Churchill was equally anxious to avoid the Allied errors committed after World War I. He opposed reparations so great that once more economic chaos and starvation would ravage Germany and once more the Western Allies would have to feed, support, and rebuild the country. But apparent American indifference, Anglo-American sympathy for the devastation and suffering the Russians had endured at German

As the Germans fell back, fighting desperate rear-guard actions, Hitler clung

hands, and the desire to meet Stalin halfway led
to accepting the $20,000,000,000 figure as a "basis
for discussion." The Soviets subsequently chose to
treat that as a confirmed agreement. Also, Churchill
did not propose to so impoverish Germany economically
and weaken it politically that it could not, in due time,
take its place with France and Britain in building a
more secure balance of power in Europe.

Roosevelt's main objective at Yalta seemed to be
to have Stalin specify when he would declare war on
Japan and to what extent his armed forces would
be committed. The President was motivated by a
variety of factors in his zeal. Diehard, to-the-last-
man Japanese resistance, and the new suicidal
kamikazes the Americans had encountered in the

to the vain hope that Britain and America would agree to a separate peace.

island war in the Pacific boded ill for the invasion of Japan. The American Chiefs of Staff had warned that invading the Japanese home islands might cost a million casualties, and that the war with Japan might be prolonged 18 months after victory in Europe. The atomic bomb, though close to completion, remained untested and could not be counted on. To shorten the war and save American lives, Roosevelt was determined to nail down Stalin's participation in the war against Japan, and therefore felt it necessary to make concessions to the Soviets. He was not deterred by the fact that, in July 1944, General Douglas MacArthur and Admiral Chester W. Nimitz, the chief commanders in the Pacific, had assured him that Japan could be brought to its knees by combined sea-air assault and blockade without invading Japan proper, and that General Henry H. Arnold, head of the Air Force, not only concurred in this opinion, but by Yalta had his B-29 "Superfortresses" bombarding the Japanese mainland from the Marianas.

In private talks with Stalin, Roosevelt agreed to the Russian's price for participation. The concessions were great. Southern Sakhalin and the Kurile Islands were to be transferred from Japan to the Soviet Union, Dairen was to be internationalized, and Outer Mongolia given permanent autonomy, which meant, in effect, recognizing that it belonged in the Soviet sphere. More important, to "safeguard the pre-eminent interest of the Soviet Union," Russia was given a lease on the naval base at Port Arthur and joint control with China of the Chinese Eastern and South Manchurian Railways, thus making it possible for Stalin effectively to dominate Manchuria. In making these concessions, not only had Roosevelt violated Chinese sovereignty, but he had violated his own and America's expressed principles about the territorial integrity and political independence of China and of eastern Europe.

Extension of Soviet influence in the latter area opened the unbridgeable chasm between East and West, and Poland was the touchstone of the issues involved. Stalin demanded that Poland's eastern frontier be the Curzon line, which the Allied Supreme Council in 1919 had determined as a fair ethnic division between Poland and the USSR, and that the Allies recognize the Communist-dominated Lublin "National Committee of Liberation" as the provisional government of Poland. Britain had gone to war against Germany to satisfy its treaty obligations with Poland, had recognized, supported and given a home to the Polish Government-in-Exile in London, and was committed to a free, independent and sovereign Poland. Not only were there 150,000 Polish troops in the British armed forces, but there were five to six million American voters of Polish extraction, who also counted in the Anglo-American calculations. For better than a year, Churchill had tried to harmonize the differences between the London Poles and the USSR, but the Poles refused to accept the Curzon line.

Aware that Red Army control of Poland might shortly deprive the London Poles of any chance of influencing Poland's future, Churchill invited their Prime Minister, Stanislaw Mikolajczyk, to come to Moscow in October 1944 to his conference with Stalin. Mikolajczyk was finally persuaded to accept the Curzon line if Stalin left Poland the Carpathian oil fields, but he could not carry the rest of the London Government-in-Exile along with him, and he then resigned.

At Yalta, the Big Three agreed to recognize the Curzon line, though Stalin refused to include Lvov and the Carpathian oil fields in the Polish boundaries.

They also agreed to compensate Poland with substantial chunks of German territory, giving Poland all East Prussia south and west of Königsberg, the Baltic ports of Danzig and Stettin, and extending Poland's western frontier to the Oder and Neisse Rivers. Though Stalin was quite willing for the Poles to move to the western Neisse, Churchill and Roosevelt thought the eastern Neisse was far west enough. Final agreement among them on Polish western boundaries was postponed

The basic issue, however, was not Poland's geographical boundaries, but the boundaries of its freedom, independence and sovereignty, and these were indissolubly bound up with the formation of a truly representative provisional government. As Churchill stressed, "Poland must be mistress in her own house and captain of her own soul." But this was precisely what the Russians did not want. They declared in favor of an "enlarged" Lublin "National Committee of Liberation" for a provisional government, and agreed to add several London Poles to it. The Anglo-American Allies at first refused to recognize the Lublin Committee and proposed a new government drawn from all major democratic political parties, from Poland and London, and which would represent a majority.

After long wrangling, Soviet persistence, obstinacy and clarity of purpose once more carried the day. Aided and abetted by imprecise language, the final joint Yalta protocol in effect provided Allied recognition of the Lublin Committee as the Provisional Government of Poland. The only change was that instead of having it "enlarged," as Stalin had originally suggested, the Allies accepted the term "reorganized." The verbal change meant little and left the Soviets all they needed to keep Poland under their sway.

All the Big Three agreed that free elections based

on universal suffrage and a secret ballot should be held as soon as possible. The Soviets agreed to Allied supervisions and estimated that they might take place within a month, but Molotov refused to give written guarantees that the Anglo-American ambassadors would be permitted to supervise the Polish elections.

In spite of the many conflicts left unresolved and the clashes of interest just beneath the surface of the negotiations, most of the Yalta Conference's participants came away feeling that the meeting was the "high tide of Big Three unity." But the Western Allies had negotiated in good faith and in the spirit of comradeship-in-arms and the Soviets had not.

Clearing the Rhineland

The final Anglo-American offensive against the Reich was planned in three stages: destroying the bulk of the German armies, which Hitler had concentrated in the Rhineland; crossing the Rhine, followed by a double envelopment of the Ruhr; and finally overrunning the heart of Germany and linking up with the Red Army. Facing General Eisenhower's 85 Allied divisions were 82 German ones, understrength and demoralized by the Ardennes failure, but with their backs to the Rhine, resolutely fighting back. Their position had been worsened by Hitler's decision in February to relieve Rundstedt and put Field Marshal Albert Kesselring in command. Behind the armies, the Vaterland was a shambles. Allied planes had blitzed war industries, transport and communication networks, and the synthetic oil industry particularly. With most of its coal lost or imperilled, so that little of it could be used for synthetic fuel, and all of its natural oil resources overrun, only 25 per cent of the oil and 15 per cent of the

A dead German SS trooper killed by American machine-gun fire lies in the river as infantrymen of the 26th Division hurry across under enemy fire.

A glider heads down as Anglo-American airborne troops vault the Rhine. (Below) The Remagen Bridge which was captured before it could be blown.

The Third Reich died in flames. (Above) A tank-infantry team moves into burning Wernberg. (Right) A patrol picks its way through the roofless ruins of what was once Waldenburg.

gasoline produced in spring of 1944 was now available to the German Armed Forces.

Strategic and policy differences still seriously divided the Allies. The British wanted the offensive concentrated in the north. Underlying this insistence on a "narrow" thrust with Montgomery's 21st Army Group across the Rhine and into the Westphalian plain was British fear that the Russians, already on the Oder, might break through to the North Sea ports and naval bases while the Allies, moving forward on a broad front, cleared the Rhineland.

On the other hand, the Americans believed the enemy had been so weakened by the Ardennes offensive and by the Russian victories in the east that a broad front assault would smash German resistance

Even the last days of combat in Germany brought heavy casualties. Here two

altogether. Moreover, with almost all their forces west of the Rhine and almost no reserves, once the Rhineland was cleared there would be almost nothing left to keep the Allies from overrunning the German heartland. This time the Americans proved correct.

Eisenhower nevertheless agreed to make Montgomery's the main thrust across the Rhine and assigned him 37 divisions, including the U. S. Ninth Army. He also allocated 25 divisions to General Bradley's 12th Army Group for a thrust in the center, while General Jacob L. Devers' 6th Army Group got the remainder for a holding action until Montgomery and Bradley were across the river.

But first the Rhineland had to be cleared. In preparation the U. S. Seventh Army and the French First

1st Army reconnaissance column vehicles burn after being caught in ambush.

Army in the south mopped up the Colmar pocket and
cleared the west bank of the Rhine from the Swiss
frontier to Strasbourg. In the north, the Canadian
First Army and the British Second pushed the Germans
from between the Maas and the Roer Rivers, and began
the assault on the Rhineland. The Germans had blown
up the Roer dams flooding the countryside, bogging
down Allied armor and equipment, and slowing the
advance. Flooding also delayed the Ninth Army's
converging attack on the right flank, so that the Germans could concentrate against the British and Canadians. Elements of 11 divisions, including the crack
First Parachute Army, were thrown at them and some
of the grimmest, bloodiest fighting of the war took
place in the Reichswald and Hochwald forests as Mont-

gomery's troops, in a half-amphibious operation, pushed the Germans back across the Rhine. Two weeks later, on February 23, when the waters had subsided, Simpson threw his Ninth Army into the battle and by mid-March the Allies had cleared the west bank of the Rhine from Nijmegen to Düsseldorf.

On Simpson's right flank, Hodges' First Army, which had captured the Roer dams, drove forward and by March 7 had taken Cologne, Germany's fourth largest city. On the same day it had a stroke of luck when its

With the British the northern arm of a pincers and the Americans the south-

9th Armored Division captured the Ludendorff Bridge at Remagen. Hitler had ordered every bridge over the Rhine destroyed but only at the last minute, so that supplies could flow forward and troops could, if necessary, retreat. Somehow, the Nazis failed to blow up the Remagen Bridge and Hitler shot four officers he held responsible. General Hodges quickly put five divisions of his First Army across to the east bank of the Rhine and these swiftly fanned out, seized the high ground commanding the river, cut the Frankfort-Cologne

ern, the Allies made a vast pocket of the Ruhr and took 325,000 prisoners.

autobahn (super-highway), and extended the bridge-head to a length of 29 miles and a width of 9 miles before the Ludendorff Bridge collapsed into the Rhine.

On Hodges' right, Patton sent his Third Army hurtling through Trier and joined the First Army on the Rhine at Andernach between Remagen and Coblenz. All the Rhineland north of the Moselle River was now under Allied control. What remained was the Saar-Palatinate triangle to the south. Patton drove across the Moselle striking against its north flank, while Patch's Seventh Army plunged through the Siegfried line against its southern flank. Between them they had cleared all the triangle by March 27, and the Allied armies all along the line had closed on the Rhine.

While Eisenhower held the First Army back in the Remagen bridgehead waiting Montgomery's assault in the north, Patton slipped a whole division across the Rhine on the night of March 22 at Oppenheim, between Mainz and Mannheim, and on March 23, Montgomery launched the major strike at Wesel. In a beautifully planned and prepared assault, preceded by intensive aerial and withering artillery bombardment, and coordinated with an air drop of 2 divisions of 14,000 airborne troops behind the German lines, Montgomery threw four divisions over the Rhine and smashed through the German defenses. Simultaneously, the First and Third Armies were unleashed from the Remagen and Oppenheim bridgeheads and surged forward. The Ninth Army cut around the northern edge of the Ruhr while the First went around the southern edge; they joined at Lippstadt and the Ruhr was encircled. In spite of heavy casualties in the Rhineland fighting, the Germans had extricated the bulk of their armies and now they were trapped in the Ruhr. By April 18, the Allies had cut the Ruhr pocket to shreds and

Boys — like the fourteen-year-olds above — were thrown into the battle in the closing days to make good German losses. These youngsters were taken prisoners defending a Rhine crossing. Most veterans of the old, once invincible Wehrmacht (below) were now wounded, dead, or in Allied prisons.

An aerial view of thousands of recently captured German prisoners-of-war.

325,000 troops were forced to surrender; their commander, Field Marshal Model, loyal Nazi to the end, committed suicide. With the Saar and Silesia already overrun, the loss of the Ruhr left Germany without a major industrial area still under its control. Moreover, the Ruhr pocket had destroyed almost all the effective fighting forces facing the western Allies; there was virtually no resistance between the Allies and Berlin.

Montgomery sent the Canadians wheeling northward into Holland, and the British Second Army racing for the Baltic. Bradley sent Simpson, Hodges, and Patton plunging across the center of Germany for the Elbe. Devers sent Patch across the Rhine on March 26, the French First Army across on April 1, and then directed them southeast, the Seventh through Munich to Salzburg, the First French Stuttgart and the Swiss frontier.

The Ultimate Horror

As the Allied armies dashed through Germany, they not only found the Nazi gold hoard ($250,000,000,000 in gold bars, gold coins, and various currencies, buried 1200 feet deep in a salt mine) they found things they had never thought to see—and would never forget. R. W. Thompson, war correspondent of the London Sunday Times, describes Bergen-Belsen:

The blue smoke of many fires hangs thickly in the pine woods along the road from Winsen to Belsen. In the clearings the young corn is green and all the loveliness of spring, of budding life, is in the air, and the smouldering grasses of the pine woods bring a wonderful tang to the nostrils so that you expand your chest and feel your youth still in you, and are glad to be alive. Then suddenly a new tang creeps into the odours of burning. It is the stench of death. It is the stench from the great charnel-house our armies have overrun so that all mankind shall know—and this time neither to balk nor forget—the appalling crime Hitler and the Nazis have done against humanity, against the very basis of life and faith itself. . . .

I began the unforgettable walk that you must read about. At first it was little worse than a kind of enormous hutted camp with here and there the wooden towers where the guards had watched. The whole enormous area hidden in lovely pine woods divided into barbed-wire enclosures each containing about thirty long huts to house, on military standards, less than 50 men. Here the inmates, men, women and children, were new, but recently brought in. For the first time for days there was water, and for the first time for weeks these people were washing themselves and their clothes. The only odd thing was that here and there men and women were excreting—just casually anywhere. There is no sanitation in this hell in the woods.

And now before my eyes was the slow destruction of human beings, stripped of all human dignity, forced down to the level of the beasts, and so to die in utter ruin. This thing, this hell far beyond the wild dreams of Dante, holds some 60,000 souls—souls! These are not souls, these tragic travesties of humanity that sit and rot in their own excrement, these things that were human once, reduced now to skeleton death by slow deliberate starvation, but first stripped of all remnants of human dignity so that in truth they are dead before they die. By the barbed wire lie the dead, some bits of clothing, others naked, men, women and children, almost unrecognisable as the remains of human kind though they died but an hour since. . . .

They lie down and they die. Now deep into the

camp the dead lie in bundles, neat bundles, grotesque limbs in terrible positions. Here is a small cart loaded with a dozen corpses of men, women and children, the faces like parchment tight against the skulls. They are only just dead. A brown stocking is limply around a leg that a small black garter less than 4 inches diameter cannot clasp. A shock of auburn hair crowns the dead face of this woman that stares sightless to the blue sky. The normal world of life is receding. Horror is not yet too deep for an individual to mean something. This woman had a life, a purpose, was beloved of someone. But now the dead are in hundreds, the dead, the living and the near-living. The dead in small bundles of threes or fours under the shadow of the pines, the dying in attitudes of sleep by the roadside, some dying peacefully, some suddenly sitting up chattering. Here a woman sits with eyes round in deep sockets, and a younger woman tries to quiet her babbling. She is babbling like a grotesque travesty of a child. If you did not know, she might be asking for a toy to play with, but she is asking for death. . . .

And so slowly the Chaplain takes me to the great burial ground where our soldiers are scooping pits with bulldozers to accommodate all this dead and putrefying human wreckage, deliberately, slowly, brought to this pass by Adolf Hitler and the German race. Morning and night the heavy truck with its trailers brings its cargoes of bodies to the great pits. Stand with me at the brink of this death pit. It is my job, your job, and the world's job. It is about 30 feet deep, but you cannot see how deep because it is nearly filled now with human bodies, littered together in the embrace of death. Here are girls, boys, men, women, naked, half-naked, upside down, sideways, all ways, some staring up to the sky, others with their heads

The advance liberated many concentration camps. (Below) An inmate of Belsen.

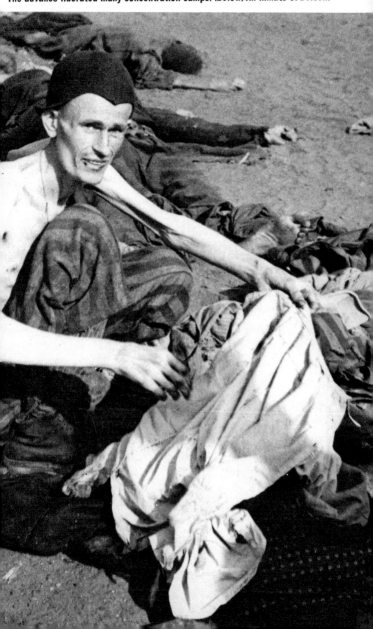

Two clergymen hold a service over a mass grave at Belsen.
The threat of epidemic made mass burials necessary.

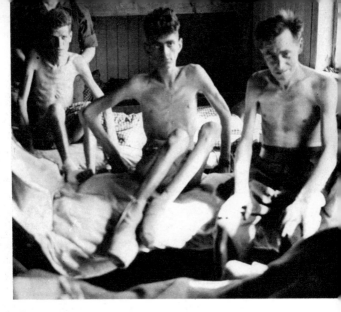

Prisoners-of-war fared little better at Nazi hands. English PWs from Stalag II-B (above) show their malnutrition plainly. (Below) Russians used as forced labor turn on a Nazi guard. They beat him badly until he was rescued by British troops.

buried in human remains. So stare in silence and let this crime beyond expression sink in. Across the sandy clearing is the incinerator, but it ran out of petrol. A rough record by the chief burner of bodies records seventeen thousand burned last month. They say each body was roughly clubbed as it went in, for there is so little difference between the dead and the near-dead. There is no difference in the faces even. . . .

Germany was deadly for me. I loathed it. It clamped down upon my spirit. . . . I found it difficult to speak to Germans at all. I used to walk through crowds of them—civilians or prisoners—as though they weren't there, yet feeling a kind of flaming wall around me. . . . The monstrous thing changed me. My outlook on life has changed—or developed—so that all my thoughts on social, political, and economic affairs have crystallised. I am now a complete idealist. I have given up all the "isms." I believe in the human spirit above all things, and that only by a change of heart can civilization be saved.

For although it is the Germans who have done this thing, it is not only the Germans who can do it. Prisoners of Germans did it to other prisoners. Mankind can do this thing to mankind.

Red Army in Germany

In January, the Russians launched their all-out offensive all along the central front. It began on the twelfth with Koniev smashing out of the Sandomierz-Baranov bridgehead over the Vistula and was followed two days later by Zhukov, on his right, breaking out of bridgeheads near Warsaw. Together they tore the entire German Vistula defense line apart and, with no natural barrier in their way, raced across the Polish

Russian engineers carrying explosives work their way towards a building which

plains for Germany. Zhukov outflanked and encircled Warsaw, took it from the rear on January 17, and drove straight for the Oder River. Koniev seized abandoned Cracow on the nineteenth, then sent his army rolling into Silesia. By mid-February, Zhukov was on the Oder at Frankfort and Kuestrin, only 45 miles from Berlin, and Koniev was on the Neisse, 60 miles beyond Breslau and only about 100 miles from Prague. It was a magnificent victory for the Red Army and a catastrophic defeat for Germany. In three weeks the Russians had gone 275 miles, cleared most of Poland, and overrun the coal fields and industries of Silesia, the last German industrial basin relatively undamaged by Allied bombing.

In March, Zhukov turned to reduce the fortresses and pockets he had bypassed and left encircled in his rear. Together with Rokossovski he also set out to clear his extended and exposed right flank. They sent columns north which fought their way to the mouth of the Oder, taking Stettin, and which cut the German defenders

was converted into a stronghold. (Right) Red infantry pours into Germany.

into pockets and then crushed them. After taking Gdynia and Danzig at the end of March, the Nazis had only three pockets left on the Baltic coast east of the Oder: Courland, Königsberg, and one centered on Kolberg in Pomerania. On April 9, after fierce and bloody street fighting, Königsberg fell to Vassilevsky. Once the Kolberg pocket was eliminated, the Russians had a coherent north-south line along the Oder and Neisse Rivers, and Zhukov and Koniev had two new armies free for smashing the Oder line.

On the Danubian front, after fierce German counter-attacks and seven weeks of savage house-to-house fighting, encircled Budapest fell to Malinovsky and Tolbukhin on February 13. Quickly redeploying their armies, the Russian Marshals sent their spearheads in a giant pincers toward Vienna. Striking up on both sides of Lake Balaton, Tolbukhin wheeled up toward Vienna from the southeast while Malinovsky drove through northwest Hungary and Slovakia toward the Austrian capital. On April 3, Malinovsky took Bratislava

Russian troops surging towards Berlin march prisoners past a dead Nazi. The Germans feared the advancing Russians (below) more than either American or British troops.

and Tolbukhin, Wiener Neustadt. Four days later their advanced columns were ringing the outskirts of Vienna. After bitter street fighting, the city fell on April 13.

As Allied military victories mounted on both fronts, so did political differences growing out of the unresolved contradiction into which Roosevelt and Churchill had stumbled at Yalta. On one hand they promised Stalin that Soviet security would be protected by "friendly" governments in neighboring countries; on the other, they favored democratic elections which made such "friendly" governments impossible. Nowhere in Eastern Europe could a Russian-sponsored or Communist regime gain genuine popular support; free and unfettered elections were far more likely to produce actively anti-Russian and anti-Communist governments.

Stalin had taken his "percentage agreement" with Churchill and the Yalta accord to mean Anglo-American recognition of Soviet dominance of the area. The President and Prime Minister had not protested Soviet absorption of Baltic countries and had also accepted Communist domination of Yugoslavia and Albania.

Everywhere, now, Stalin used the presence of the Red Army, armed Communist minorities and Soviet political pressure to guarantee "friendly" governments in Eastern Europe. By spring a deadlock on Eastern Europe had been reached between East and West. In the face of futile Anglo-American protest, the Russians had set up Communist-dominated regimes in Romania, Bulgaria, and Poland; and Russian-sponsored but non-Communist coalition governments were installed in Austria, Czechoslovakia, and Hungary. Only in Finland was the nation's sovereignty and independence relatively untrammeled. With or without Anglo-American formal acknowledgment, the Russians had staked out their claim to replace the German empire in the East.

The Allies Triumphant

After conquering Rome in June 1944, Field Marshal Alexander pressed the Germans hard, keeping them from transferring two of their best armies from Italy to either Western or Eastern front. Though Alexander's forces had been seriously weakened by diverting General Patch's Seventh Army to the invasion of Southern France, he drove almost 250 miles from the Gustav line to the Gothic line in two months of fighting, and by the end of August his armies had closed on the Arno River's south bank. Kesserling had skillfully managed to pull his troops back to the 180-mile-long Gothic line, a series of powerful fortifications 20 miles deep, which ran north of Lucca across the Apennines

On the secondary Italian front, Imperial and American troops fought through mud and mountains, keeping two Nazi armies engaged as they slowly drove on to liberate Hitler's ex-ally.

to the Adriatic Coast below Pesaro. In September, the Allied armies stormed the Gothic line, but rains and winter weather, unfavorable terrain, and dogged German resistance stopped General Mark W. Clark's Fifth Army just short of Bologna and the British Eighth Army just beyond Rimini.

The combination of Red Army military successes, Soviet political intransigence and violations of the Yalta Agreement also divided the British and Americans. Again, it was war as a political instrument versus war as purely military strategy, and "narrow thrust" versus "broad thrust." Concerned about increasing Russian hostility and the tightening Soviet hold on Eastern Europe, Churchill wanted to "shake hands with the Russians as far to the east as possible." Consequently, he wanted General Eisenhower to push ahead and overrun as much territory as he could to strengthen the Anglo-American hand in the peace table bargaining. In this way he hoped not only to wait until Russia's intentions, now in serious question, were clarified, but also to force them to honor their commitments. Politically and symbolically, Churchill considered Berlin the prime target. The Russians already acted as if they alone had fought the entire war and won all the victories. Churchill saw the importance of capturing the capital of Hitler's Reich instead of leaving it to be liberated by the Russians and he thought, too, that German resistance would collapse militarily once their capital surrendered.

Eisenhower, on the other hand, thought Berlin of no military importance and did not wish to risk the 100,000 casualties he thought storming it might entail. Besides he was more than 200 miles from Berlin, and Zhukov less than 40. Also, knowing that the occupation zones had already been decided on at Yalta by the political leaders, Eisenhower could not see the sense in overrunning more territory to the east when he would only have to turn it back to the Russians to whose zone it had been allocated.

In addition, Eisenhower's Intelligence reports told of Nazi plans for a fanatical last-ditch battle in the "Alpine Fortress" or "National Redoubt" in the Bavarian Alps which they hoped would prolong the war and ease the peace terms. To prevent this stand, Eisenhower decided to shift his main thrust away from Berlin, where few troops stood in his way, to clear his flank on the south and destroy German concentrations in the "National Redoubt."

At Yalta, Eisenhower had been given permission to coordinate battle plans directly with the Russians without going through the Combined Chiefs of Staff. In these last stages of the battle, decisions might have to be made quickly to avoid accidental clashes between the advancing Anglo-American and Russian armies, and Eisenhower's hands had to be free. On March 28, Eisenhower notified Marshal Stalin, who was also Commander-in-Chief of the Red Armies, that his Armies were going to strike for Dresden, not for Berlin, and asked what the Russian plans were. Stalin, of course, was quite agreeable, but Churchill and the British Chiefs of Staff were angry because they thought Eisenhower had exceeded his authority in dealing directly with Stalin, and also because they did not want the axis of assault shifted southward. They wanted to push to the Baltic in the north, to Berlin in the center, and as far beyond the Elbe River as they could all along the line. And they put little credence in the reports of a "Twilight of the Gods" in the "National Redoubt." Churchill tried to persuade Roosevelt to overrule the decision, but both the President and the U. S. Chiefs

Robert Capa's Leipzig sequence: (top) preparing a machine-gun; (above) firing; seconds before being hit (right). Moments later a new gunner took over.

With the end of the war only weeks away, the British attack near Lubeck.

of Staff backed Eisenhower to the hilt.

Once more a fateful disagreement divided the Allied leaders on how military and political aims in Europe could be coordinated. As he had failed to persuade the American President to favor an invasion of the "soft underbelly" of Europe to prevent the installation of Soviet power in the Balkans, so now Churchill failed once again in his attempt to prevail on Roosevelt to have American armies plunge ahead and forestall Soviet hegemony in Central Europe.

The Death of Franklin D. Roosevelt

Though continued pressure from the British and continuing Soviet antagonism might have changed Roosevelt's mind, on April 12, the President suffered a cerebral hemorrhage at his retreat in Warm Springs, Georgia, and within a matter of hours he was dead. All over the world, leaders and common people alike, mourned the great symbol of freedom and democracy. The next day the President's name appeared simply in the lists of latest military casualties in the newspapers; undoubtedly the great burden he had borne during the war had shortened his life. Franklin D. Roosevelt had steered the nation through the most trying days of the war, but he had been cut off when profound political divisions in the Allied camp were still unreconciled and the shape of the peace was still unclear. At this military and political climax of the war, an unprepared and as yet uninformed Vice-President, Harry S. Truman, took his place at the helm, but it could not be expected that, at first, he would or could do more than continue the policies Roosevelt had set before him.

With the victory he fought for in sight, FDR died and the nation mourned.

Death of the Tyrant

In the meantime, in the face of the impending collapse of his Thousand Year Reich, Hitler went about trying to pull Germany down around his ears. He proclaimed:

If the war is lost, the German nation will also perish. This fate is inevitable. There is no need to take into consideration the basic requirements of the people for continuing even a most primitive existence.... Those who will remain after the battle are those who are inferior; for the good will have fallen. And he issued orders to scorch the earth against the invaders. For a change, German generals and industrialists combined and refused to carry out such an order.

In April, the Reich crumbled everywhere. Anglo-American armies closed to the Elbe-Mulde line and were held there for two weeks by Eisenhower waiting for the Red Army. Zhukov smashed east from his Kuestrin bridgehead across the Oder, and Koniev wheeled north from the Neisse, both converging on Berlin. By April 25 they had encircled and besieged the city. There, Hitler personally conducted a futile and fanatic defense from a deep underground bunker beneath the Reich Chancellery.

Finally, on April 30, with the Russians closing in, and after having married his mistress, Eva Braun, Hitler gave her poison and shot himself. Also in the Führerbunker, Goebbels, the evil propaganda genius of the Third Reich, poisoned his wife and six children before taking the final dose himself. When it was over, Nazi henchmen burned their bodies.

After 12 days of savage struggle, the capital of the Third Reich finally fell to Red Army columns led by Zhukov and Koniev on May 2.

The End in Germany

Hodges' First Army captured Magdeburg and Leipzig and made the first junction with Koniev's 1st Ukrainian Army at Torgau on the Elbe on April 25. Patton's Third Army rolled across the Czech border on May 5 and could easily have captured all of Bohemia without danger of clashing with Koniev's troops 70 miles from Prague. Eisenhower informed the Russians that Patton could push on to Prague, but the Soviet High Command replied that his army should halt on the line Budejovice-Pilsen-Karlsbad. Though Churchill insisted that Anglo-American liberation of Prague and western Czechoslovakia was politically of first importance in determining the postwar status of the country and of its neighbors, and though the Czech Underground rose in revolt and broadcast a plea for Allied help, Eisenhower felt he had to abide by his agreement with the Russians, and ordered Patton's columns halted. The Germans crushed the Czech rebellion and the liberation of Prague was left to the Red Army.

Eisenhower did, however, assign units from the Ninth Army to Montgomery in the north so that the British were able to cross the Elbe, capture Lübeck and Kiel, and seal off the Germans in Denmark, and beat the Russians to the Baltic by a scant 24 hours, meeting the onrushing Rokossovski's columns at Wismar between Lübeck and Rostock.

In the south the Americans did not meet the fanatical underground resistance campaign in the "Alpine Fortress" they had been led to expect. The Seventh Army stopped at Innsbruck on May 3 to await the Russians coming up from the southeast, and General Patch sent Seventh Army spearheads down through the Brenner Pass for a junction with the victorious Allied

In a Berlin bunker Hitler committed suicide. His grave remains unknown.

Mussolini and his mistress Clara Petacci are hung by the heels in Milan.

Russians and Americans linked up and embraced (above). A stern Montgomery receives peace delegates from the north German armies. The German aim was to surrender their troops to the West rather than to the Red Army. The Allies held out for a single surrender and on May 7 it was completed. General Jodl (below, center) signed for the Reich, General Walter Bedell Smith (below, right), for the US. The war in Europe was over.

armies in the northern sectors of Italy.

There, on April 9, the U. S. Fifth Army and the British Eighth Army had launched their final offensive, broken through the line of the Po, and the German defenses had collapsed in front of them. The British streaked around the head of the Adriatic to meet Tito's Partisans near Trieste while the Americans dashed to the Brenner Pass to cut off the German escape route, and simultaneously pushed west to meet French troops driving from the Riviera. Italian Partisans organized a rising on April 25, seizing major cities, among them Milan, Turin, Genoa, and Venice, and on April 28, they discovered Mussolini and his mistress, Clara Petacci, near Lake Como, trying to escape to Switzerland. Relentlessly, they shot them down and took their corpses to Milan, to be strung up by the heels in a public

square and abused and mutilated by the violence of the people Il Duce had long oppressed.

The situation of the Germans was obviously hopeless. In their desperation the Germans now tried to negotiate a separate military surrender with the Western Allies to keep the bulk of their troops from falling into Russian hands. But the Anglo-American Allies rejected the various Nazi overtures, refusing anything but unconditional surrender to all Allies simultaneously. On May 7, the new head of the Reich, Grand Admiral Karl Doenitz, finally capitulated and the unconditional surrender document was signed with all the Allies at General Eisenhower's headquarters at Reims, to be

In New York City, cheering soldiers, sailors and airmen marched up Broadway

effective the next day. A second surrender ceremony took place in shattered Berlin on May 8. This was the one the Russian people were informed was the actual surrender.

After five and a half years the war in Europe was over. Millions lay dead, permanently disabled and wandered rootless and homeless over a continent that had been turned into a shambles. The Thousand Year Reich had fallen and the leading Nazis and top German generals were either dead or in Allied hands, but all Eastern Europe was once again under the control of a single totalitarian power: Communist Russia had replaced Nazi Germany as overlord of an empire.

to celebrate. But all knew that the war with Japan still raged on in the Pacific.

Victory in the Pacific

Saipan

By June 1944, the Marshalls had been long secured, the end of the New Guinea campaign was in view, and Truk was all but choked off. The Americans now launched a two-pronged offensive to breach Japan's second island defense ring. While MacArthur's troops were to leapfrog from New Guinea to Morotai, Nimitz's forces were to take the Marianas and Palaus; then both would converge on the Philippines. Some 1350 miles south of Tokyo, the Marianas were a chain of 17 islands, but only the four southernmost—Guam, Tinian, Rota, and Saipan—were strategically important. Japan had taken most of the islands from Germany during World War I and had their conquest formalized by a League Mandate. Guam, purchased by the U. S. in 1899, had been captured by the Japanese after Pearl Harbor.

With advanced naval and air bases in the Marianas, Nimitz could strike west at the Palaus and Philippines and north against Japan's last defense perimeter—the Bonin and Ryukyu Islands—and ultimately against the Japanese home islands. Capturing the Marianas not only cut off Truk's last supply and communication route from the north, but also provided airfields within striking range of Tokyo. A Japanese offensive in China had forced the U. S. 14th Air Force out of its advanced air bases; the Marianas could provide more secure and closer bases from which the new B-29 Superfortresses could bomb Japan proper.

But if the Marianas had advantages to those who held them, they had great disadvantages for those who had to assault them. They combined the difficulties of a fringing coral reef, rugged and extensive terrain well suited for defense, some 3000 native Chamorros and

A gull-winged Navy F4U Corsair fires a salvo of rockets in the Pacific.

a large and loyal Japanese civilian population. Nimitz sent Task Force 58 under Admiral Raymond Spruance with 535 ships, 2000 aircraft, and 300,000 soldiers, sailors, and Marines to seize Saipan, Tinian, and Guam. For the Saipan assault, the 2nd Marine Division, veterans of Guadalcanal and Tarawa, and the 4th Marine Division, veterans of the Marshalls, were joined by the Army's 27th Infantry Division, veterans of Makin and Eniwetok, some 77,500 troops in all. On June 15, only 9 days after the Normandy landings, they stormed ashore to meet a murderous hail of fire.

The Japanese had not yet completed Saipan's defenses because they had given priority to the Palaus, where, due to MacArthur's May 26 landing on Biak, they expected the first strike, but the 32,000-man Japanese garrison under Lieutenant General Jiro Saito fought a skillful, stubborn battle. From blockhouses, pillboxes, machine-gun nests, and a maze of trenches and dugouts, savage artillery, mortar and machine-gun fire made soldiers and Marines pay in blood for every advance. Differences in soldier and Marine training, tactics and leadership created further difficulties and a major inter-service row when commanding Marine Lieutenant General "Howlin' Mad" Smith relieved Army Major General Ralph Smith as commander of the 27th Division because the 27th's slow advance exposed the inside flanks of the Marine divisions.

It took two weeks of ferocious fighting before the Americans had sliced the island in two, overrun the lower third of it, and seized the two major air fields and the strategic heights of Mount Tapotchau. It took two weeks more before they had shoved the remnants of the Japanese garrison into a small salient on the northern tip of the island. On the Fourth of July, after losing the island capital of Garapan, the Japanese

Marines with a flame-throwing tank (above) move up during an attack on Saipan. Stiff Japanese resistance and banzai charges were repulsed, sometimes with artillery fuses cut at zero. (Below) Unable to face their defeat, the Japanese soldiers chose suicide rather than surrender.

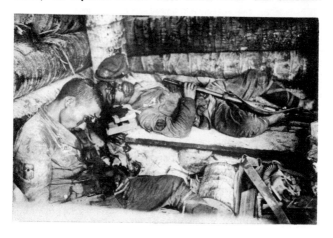

struck out in two final suicidal banzai charges between July 6 and 8 which effectively brought the battle to an end. On July 8, after stopping the banzai charges and after 25 days of slaughter, organized resistance ended, but mopping-up operations continued for a year. More than 3000 Americans died in the battle and almost 13,500 were wounded and missing. Japanese dead numbered 25,400, with more than 1700 taken prisoner and 10,250 civilians captured. On July 11 and 12, these Japanese civilians added a gory postscript to an already bloody campaign. Robert Sherrod gives an eyewitness account of the holocaust:

Some of the Jap civilians went through considerable ceremony before snuffing out their lives. In one instance Marines watched in astonishment as three women sat on the rocks, leisurely, deliberately combing their long, black hair—much after the fashion of Leonidas and his Spartans before their last stand at Thermopylae. Finally, the women joined hands and walked slowly into the sea.

But the most ceremonious, by all odds, were the 100 Japs on the rocks who bowed to the Marines watching them from the cliff. Then they stripped off their clothes and bathed in the sea. Thus refreshed, they put on new clothes and spread a huge Jap flag on a smooth rock. Then the leader distributed hand grenades. One by one, as the pins were pulled, the Japs blew their insides out. . . .

I remember one woman in khaki trousers and a white, polka-dot blouse, with her black hair streaming in the water. I'm afraid every time I see that kind of blouse, I'll think of that girl. There was another one, nude, who had drowned herself while giving birth to a baby. The baby's head had entered the world, but that was all of him. A small boy of four or five had drowned with his arm firmly clenched around the neck of a Jap soldier; the two bodies rocked crazily in the waves. I've seen literally hundreds in the water. . . .

Some Jap soldiers had fled to the reef, several hundred yards offshore. Hensley had taken a detachment of amphibious tractors to fetch them. As the amphtracs approached, one of the Japs, apparently an officer, drew his sword. The six men with him knelt on the coral rocks, and the officer started methodically to slice off their heads. Four heads had rolled into the sea before the amphtracs closed in. Then the officer, sword in hand, charged the amphtracs. Hensley's men turned their machine guns on him and the two remaining men.

The military commander, General Saito, and Vice-Admiral Nagumo, commander of the force which bombed Pearl Harbor, both committed suicide in the last days of the battle.

The Philippine Sea

The Marianas invasion posed such a serious threat that the Japanese High Command could not let it go by without intervening. While the fighting raged on Saipan, Admiral Soemu Toyoda, new commander of the Japanese Combined Fleet, sent his First Mobile Fleet under Vice-Admiral Jisaburo Ozawa to smash it. Ozawa's fleet was made up of 5 aircraft carriers, 4 light carriers, 5 battleships, 11 heavy cruisers, 2 light cruisers, and 28 destroyers, but it faced an even more formidable force in Spruance's Task Force 58, which had 7 carriers, 8 light carriers, 7 battleships, 8 heavy cruisers, 13 light cruisers, and 69 destroyers. Not only did Spruance have superiority in every naval category except heavy cruisers, but he had a critical 2-1 su-

The battle in the Pacific was to knock out carriers like the Zuiho (abov

periority in airplanes, 956 to 473. Ozawa hoped to equalize this aerial disparity by using land-based planes from the Palaus, Guam, Tinian, Yap, and Truk, but his air reinforcements had at the last minute been sent to bolster resistance to MacArthur's invasion of Biak. Even in ships Toyoda was apparently reluctant to commit his full strength to a decisive battle. However

Japanese plane downed by flak; (below) a merchant ship sunk.

powerful Ozawa's battle squadron was, it was not large enough to do the job assigned to it and it was too large for the Japanese to afford to lose.

In the greatest carrier battle of the war, three days running, from June 18-20, 1944, in which once more surface vessels did not fire a shot, the Japanese suffered an overwhelming defeat. Vice-Admiral Marc A.

Mitscher, in command of the Fast Carrier Forces, gave Japan's naval aviation a blow from which it never recovered in a two-day air battle which American fliers dubbed the "Great Marianas Turkey Shoot." Mitscher then launched his planes against Ozawa's fleet and, in combination with Admiral Charles Lockwood's submarines, which had sent two Japanese carriers to the bottom on their way to the battle and done yeoman reconnaissance work as well, sank a third carrier and a light carrier, damaged two other light carriers and several other ships. American losses were 130 planes, 76 pilots, and 3 warships slightly damaged.

Because the remainder of Ozawa's fleet escaped, Spruance was severely criticized for excessive caution. However, his primary assignment was protecting the Saipan landings and in doing just that he made possible the conquest of the Marianas.

Guam and Tinian

Invading Guam was delayed until the Japanese fleet had been driven off and victory on Saipan assured. Then, after 17 days of naval and aerial bombardment, the longest "softening up" of the war, the 3rd Marine Division, the Army 77th Infantry Division and the 1st Marine Provisional Brigade, all under Major General Roy Geiger's command, stormed ashore on two almost uncontested beaches. But once ashore they met more than 18,500 Japanese troops under Lieutenant General Sho Takashima on terrain much like that on Saipan and as fiercely defended. They also met the same wild, drunken banzai charges. Here, Marine Corps combat correspondent Alvin M. Josephy described the night counterattack of July 25 on Guam:

At about 3 A.M. a rifleman named Martinez heard a

swishing of grass out ahead of him, like men moving about. Then he noticed the pang of pieces of metal hitting each other and a busy stirring in the darkness that made him uneasy. He peered into the mist but was unable to see anything. Then, as he listened, other things happened. A barrage of hand grenades flew through the darkness and exploded behind him. . . .

At the same time an orange signal flare shot up from the Japanese lines. A sing song voice shouted into the night, and an avalanche of screaming forms bounded suddenly into view. With their bayonets gleaming in the light of sudden flares, they charged toward the Marine foxholes, throwing grenades and howling: "Ban-zai-ai!" like a pack of animals.

All along the line the enemy attack was on. Red tracer bullets flashed through the blackness. Japanese orange signal flares and American white illumination shells lit up the night like the Fourth of July, silhouetting the running forms of the enemy. On the right and the left the attack was stopped cold. As fast as the Japs came, they were mowed down by automatic rifles and machine guns. The enemy assault gradually focused on a draw where some American tanks were parked. The tanks fired their 75s at the charging masses. At first the Japs attacked the steel monsters like swarms of ants, firing their rifles at the metal sides and clambering up and over the tanks in a vain attempt to get at the crews inside. They screamed and pounded drunkenly on the turrets and locked hatches, but in their excitement they failed to damage a single tank. Finally, as if engaged in a wild game of follow-the-leader, many of them streamed past the tanks, down the draw toward the beach. . . .

By the wavering light of flares they saw one of the crew members trying to pull a Japanese bayonet out of another Marine's body. The same instant a wave of Japs appeared from nowhere and swept over both men. Three of the enemy, stopping at the silent machine gun, tried to turn it around to fire at the Marines. In their hysteria, one of them pulled the trigger before the gun was turned, and the bullets sprayed a group of Japs racing across the top of the ridge. Finally the Japs tried to lift the entire gun on its mount and turn the whole thing. A Marine automatic rifleman blasted them with his BAR, and the Japs dropped the gun. Two of them fell over the bodies of the Marine crew. A third pulled out a grenade and, holding it to his head, blew himself up. A moment later another band of Japs appeared. Again, several paused at the gun and tried to swing the heavy weapon around. They had almost succeeded, when from the darkness, a lone, drunken Jap raced headlong at them, tripped several feet away over a body and flew through the air. There was a blinding flash as he literally blew apart. He had been a human bomb, carrying a land mine and a blast charge on his waist. . . .

At about 0600, three hours after the enemy attack, had begun, a last wave of Japs charged over the top of the hill. It was the wildest, most drunken group of all, bunched together, howling, stumbling and waving swords, bayonets, and long poles. Some were already wounded and were swathed in gory bandages. The Marines yelled back at them and chopped them down in their mad rush. In a moment it was over. The last wave of the three-hour attack died to a man.

After 20 days of heavy, uninterrupted fighting, the 30-mile-long island was won on August 20, with casualties lighter than Saipan, but still heavy. U. S. killed and wounded amounted to more than 9100, more than 1900 of them dead. Though when the island was declared secure there were 10,971 Japanese dead and 86 prisoners, mopping up continued for a year and by mid-November 1944 casualties had reached a total of more than 17,230 Japanese killed and some 460 prisoners-of-war.

When the battle for Saipan was over, elements of the 2nd and 4th Marine Divisions crossed the two-and-a-half-mile strait to Tinian on July 24 in what many consider the "perfectly planned and almost faultlessly executed" amphibious assault in the Pacific war. With a supply and reinforcement base handy on Saipan, complete command of sea and air, and artillery on Saipan which could rake Tinian with shell-fire, the Marines were able to take the island in nine days, though it was three months before it was really secured.

So serious was the fall of Saipan and the defeat in the Philippine Sea that on July 18, General Tojo's government fell, to be replaced by General Kuniaki Koiso's, but Saipan was only the precipitating factor. As early as Midway strong Japanese forces favored a negotiated peace, but victories had strengthened Tojo and the militarists' grip on the nation.

Tojo's fall did not eliminate the power of the armed services, but while they continued to work for more vigorous prosecution of the war, the Jushin, the group of ex-Prime Ministers who advised the Emperor, together with Marquis Koichi Kido, Lord Keeper of the Privy Seal, began to work behind the scenes for a compromise peace, provided the monarchy was left intact. Koiso's Cabinet, divided against itself, thus aimed at divided goals: to fight more vigorously and to seek a diplomatic opportunity to end the war.

The Palaus and Morotai

And now Nimitz and MacArthur took two more steps preliminary to invading the Philippines. On September 15, 1944, bypassing heavily defended Halmahera Island, MacArthur's troops landed on Morotai, northwest of New Guinea.

On the same day as the Morotai landings, American forces under Admiral William F. "Bull" Halsey's command, hit Peleliu in the Palaus. Halsey was now running the Third Fleet under Nimitz. The same formidable flotilla was called the Third Fleet with Halsey in command and the Fifth when Spruance was in charge. The Fast Carrier Force was the same in both as well, though designated Task Force 58 when sailing under Spruance and Task Force 38 under Halsey, but in both cases under the command of Admiral Mitscher. Having two separate staffs permitted one to conduct a campaign while the other planned the next operation.

After invasions of Yap and Truk had been reconsidered and called off, Halsey suggested that the Palaus too be bypassed, but Nimitz overruled him. Conquest of the Palaus would complete the ring around the Caroline Islands and provide bases closer to the Philippines. The 1st Marine Division, veterans of Guadalcanal and Cape Gloucester, assaulted Peleliu, and the 81st Infantry captured Angaur and Ulithi.

Though not as publicized as Iwo Jima and Tarawa, so bitter was the fighting and so heavy were the casualties suffered by the Marines on Peleliu that Samuel Eliot Morison, official U. S. Navy historian, believes that Halsey was right about bypassing the Palaus. Some 13,600 Japanese had killed 1950 Americans, wounded 8500 more, engaged more than 42,000 troops and pinned down a large naval task force.

154

The islands had to be taken. Here, Marines fight and die to take Peleliu.

Return to the Philippines

With the capture of Morotai and Peleliu, the two Allied drives — MacArthur's through the South Pacific and Nimitz's through the Central Pacific — now converged on the vital Philippines, key to Japan's inner defense perimeter. Not only was it a matter of political loyalty to liberate the Filipinos as rapidly as possible, but with the islands in American hands, Japan was cut off from all the fuel and raw material resources in Southeast Asia and the Dutch East Indies.

In August and September 1944 weak Japanese opposition to Third Fleet air sweeps convinced Halsey that the Central Philippines were ripe for invasion and that Mindanao could safely be bypassed. When military, naval, and political leaders concurred, the decision to invade Leyte was made and the date advanced to October 20. In doing so, the U. S. would land in the heart of the archipelago and drive a wedge between the 250,000 Japanese troops Field Marshal

Though each island was drenched with shellfire, it never seemed enough.

Terauchi had deployed on Luzon and Mindanao.

Preliminary to the landings, American ships and planes lashed out at Japanese bases from Marcus Island to Mindanao, from the Kuriles to Borneo, but they concentrated on Okinawa and Formosa, from whence planes and men could most easily be staged into Leyte. In the six-week "softening-up" process, Halsey's planes destroyed almost 2000 Japanese aircraft, and sank or damaged more than 450 ships, as well as leaving a train of smashed factories, airfields, and installations in their wake. Particularly in the violent air battle over Formosa from October 12 to 15 did Halsey's fliers finish the annihilation of Japanese aerial power they had begun in the Marianas' "Great Turkey Shoot."

On D-Day an armada of 700 ships brought the armies to their goal: the east coast of Leyte. General Walter Krueger's Sixth Army was MacArthur's invading force, protected by Vice-Admiral Thomas Kinkaid's Seventh Fleet, whose old battleships and escort car-

The beaches and the jungles still needed the closeup fire of the mortars.

General Douglas MacArthur making good his pledge to return to the Philippines.

riers provided gunnery support and air cover for the amphibious landings. Halsey's Third Fleet with Mitscher's fast carriers and powerful new battleships was to cover the invasion and keep it from being attacked from the sea. The landings were not very difficult and only lightly opposed. Within two days more than 100,000 troops were ashore, and MacArthur had announced: "People of the Philippines, I have returned. By the grace of Almighty God our forces stand again on Philippine soil. . . . Rally to me. Let the indomitable spirit of Bataan and Corregidor lead on. . . ."

The Japanese had long expected that the prongs of the Pacific pincers would close on the Philippines and had prepared their Sho-Go—or Victory—plan to meet that contingency. A decisive battle would have to be fought or Japan was lost. No sooner was he informed of the landings when Admiral Toyoda put the Sho plan into action. Though the Japanese Navy had not recovered from the Battle of the Philippine Sea, and its carrier plane pilots had been decimated still further over Formosa, Toyoda sent the bulk of his remaining fleet to oppose American reconquest of the Philippines.

The Sho plan was shrewdly designed to take advantage of the dispersion of the Japanese fleet, the geography of the Philippines, and aggressive American psychology. Three Japanese naval squadrons were committed. Vice-Admiral Jisaburo Ozawa's Northern Force, with 1 large carrier, 3 light carriers, 2 hybrid battleship-carriers, 5 cruisers, and 6 destroyers, would steam south from Japan to rendezvous north of Luzon. They were to be the bait to lure Halsey's Third Fleet away from the Leyte beachhead. The Center Force under Vice-Admiral Takeo Kurita, with the two giant, 68,000-ton, 18-inch gunned super-battleships, Yamato and Musashi, 5 other battleships, 11 heavy cruisers, 2 light cruisers, and 19 destroyers, would sail from Singapore into the South China Sea and through the San Bernardino Strait which separates Luzon and Samar. The Southern Force, in two separate squadrons commanded respectively by Vice-Admiral Shoji Nishimura, with 2 battleships, 1 cruiser, and 4 destroyers, and Vice-Admiral Kiyohide Shima, with 3 cruisers and 4 destroyers, were to steam through the Sulu Sea, and penetrate the Surigao Strait between Mindanao and Leyte. With Halsey chasing Ozawa far to the north, the two forces would converge on the unguarded Leyte beachhead from north and south and crush it. It was a good plan and it came within an ace of succeeding.

What ensued from October 23-27, 1944, was a decisive series of air-sea battles in the greatest naval engagement in history. The encounter opened on October 23 with two American submarines sighting Kurita's Central Force, alerting Halsey, and sinking two cruisers and damaging a third. Japanese planes then retaliated by bombing the light carrier Princeton and crippling it so badly it had to be sent to the bottom. All the next day, October 24, Halsey's planes pounded Kurita's ships in the Sibuyan Sea, sending the super-battleship Musashi to the bottom and damaging several other ships. When Kurita's squadron reversed course, Halsey was sure he had crippled it and that it was beating a retreat. Search planes had by then discovered Ozawa's carriers and Halsey, eager to smash the Japanese fleet, forgot to protect the beachhead. Though he had enough battleships and carriers to deal with Kurita and Ozawa simultaneously, he did not detach any units to cover San Bernardino Strait, but set off in pursuit of Ozawa.

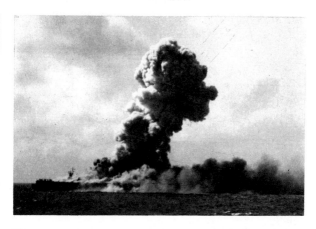

When the Americans returned to liberate the Philippines, the Japanese launched their first suicide planes (left). But the Japanese fleet was a greater threat than the Kamikazes. An enemy feint drew Halsey (lower left) and his ships north, and left only light carriers and their destroyer screen between the main Japanese fleet and the Leyte beaches. For a moment it looked as if the invasion might be smashed.

But the jeep carriers and destroyers off Samar fought so well that, incredibly, the Japanese battleships and cruisers turned back. Meanwhile, Bull Halsey's big carriers discovered the Japanese carriers without their planes and sent most of them to the bottom.

In the meantime, unaware that the Strait was now open and his northern flank uncovered, Seventh Fleet commander Kinkaid sent Rear Admiral Jesse B. Oldendorf to deal with the Japanese Southern Force expected in Surigao Strait that same night. Oldendorf had 6 old battleships, 5 of them salvaged from the Pearl Harbor debacle, 8 cruisers, 26 destroyers, and 39 torpedo (PT) boats. Late that night, Oldendorf, in a beautifully planned and executed battle, caught Nishimura's ships in a trap. With his PT boats and destroyers delivering torpedo attacks from the flanks, Oldendorf's battleships and cruisers "crossed the T" of the Japanese forces. "Crossing" or "capping the T" is a classical naval maneuver which permits the ships on the horizontal bar of the T to unmask their guns broadside against the vertical column of the enemy which can only unmask its forward batteries. Of Nishimura's squadron, only a single destroyer escaped. When Shima's group arrived in Surigao shortly thereafter, his only light cruiser was torpedoed and sunk, and after a series of accidents, Shima decided to withdraw.

During that same night Kurita's Center Force reversed its course once more and in a feat of fine seamanship navigated the treacherous and unguarded San Bernardino Strait. Early next morning, Kurita was bearing down on the beachhead and only three hours steaming away, off Samar, met the small force of American escort carriers and its destroyer screen that stood between him and the landings. The Japanese now sank 2 escort carriers, damaged 7 others, sank 3 destroyers, and damaged still another, and though the baby flattops and their destroyers fought doggedly and bravely, they were forced back toward the beachhead. Kinkaid sent frantic messages to Halsey for three hours that morning trying to get him to turn back to intercept Kurita or to send air strikes against the Japanese before they could reach the beachhead. Then, suddenly, with the landings naked and only two hours away, Kurita turned and retreated toward San Bernardino. Why he did so remains a mystery. He had intercepted a message that all Nishimura's ships but one had been sunk, and the aggressive defense of the baby carriers and their screen might have persuaded him that he was facing a more formidable enemy than he really was. In any event, with victory in his grasp, he turned and fled.

While all this was occurring, Halsey's fleet had ripped into Ozawa's squadron, Mitscher's planes sinking 4 carriers, 1 light cruiser, and 2 destroyers, and heavily damaging the 2 hybrid battleship-carriers, 2 light cruisers, and 4 destroyers. Now, Halsey, stung by a message from Nimitz asking, "Where is Task Force 34?" turned south, again leaving only some cruisers and destroyers to finish off the Japanese cripples, but not enough power to destroy the remainder of Ozawa's fleet. By the time he had returned, Kurita was through San Bernardino Strait, but Halsey's planes were still able to damage his stragglers.

The defeat in the Battle of Leyte Gulf knocked the heart out of Japan's navy. The score: 26 Japanese ships had been sent to the bottom—3 battleships, 4 carriers, 10 cruisers, and 9 destroyers—against 6 American ships lost—1 light carrier, 2 escort carriers, and 3 destroyers. It was a major and decisive American victory.

By the end of 1944, Leyte was secured but the ground fighting in the Philippines was prolonged for more than six months by bad weather, difficult terrain, and fanatical Japanese resistance. Not until

(Left) On the forgotten Burma front, Chinese Nationalists cross a river. (Above) General Joseph Stilwell, commander of the American, Burmese and Chinese troops in Burma.

July 1945, after a series of masterful combinations of amphibious assaults and parachute landings, were the rest of the Philippines liberated. For Japan it was a catastrophic defeat. Half her Navy was gone, 9,000 of her planes had been destroyed, and almost 400,000 Japanese troops were casualties. The Americans, too, had paid a heavy price, with more than 60,000 casualties and many more among the Filipino guerrillas.

In the Philippines, Americans were to see Japanese atrocities for the first time at firsthand. Everywhere, in the prison camps as well as in the countryside, there was evidence of Japanese ruthlessness. Rape, famine, disease, humiliation, and torture had deliberately been inflicted on helpless and innocent people, as well as on guerrillas, in an orgy of Bushido that neither Americans nor Filipinos would soon forget.

The Forgotten Theater

Burma was one of the most difficult theaters of the war. The terrain was an abomination of jungle, mountains, and treacherous rivers, all ridden with malaria, dysentery and scrub typhus, and almost hopeless for military operations from May to October during the monsoon season. Burma was the end of a long supply line from Britain and the United States; even from bases in India, communications with the battlefield were inadequate. In their over-all plan for war against the Axis, the Allies considered Burma a minor area of operations and assigned it virtually the last and least priorities in men and matériel. Moreover, so divided were the Allies by military, political and personal conflicts that it often seemed that Britain, China and America were fighting separate wars for opposing objectives.

For Americans the most important job in Burma was to reopen the Burma Road, which the Japanese had cut in 1942, to supply China and keep it in the war. The British, not impressed with Chinese military strength or effort, were primarily concerned with re-establishing their power in Malaya and Singapore, and with eliminating Japanese threats to restive India. Chiang Kai-shek, involved in maintaining his personal and party power, and in preparing for a postwar confrontation with Mao Tse-tung's Communists, was interested only in restoring Allied access and supplies to his government and armies. Also, he had been at war since 1937 and his armies and people were war-weary. Chinese and American aims called for a campaign in northern Burma, British aims for one in central and southern Burma.

The situation was further complicated by an unwieldy and conflicting inter-Allied command structure, and by friction between its leading personalities; between Field Marshal Archibald Wavell and Admiral Louis Mountbatten, between Mountbatten and "Vinegar Joe" Stilwell, between Stilwell and Chiang Kai-shek and Major-General Claire Chennault; and various leaders placed contrary emphasis on naval, air and ground

An American convoy on the Burma Road pushes supplies through to China.

warfare. Churchill, to avoid fighting in the terrible terrain and climate of Burma, wanted an amphibious assault on Rangoon across the Bay of Bengal. But Allied landing craft were committed to more important operations in Europe and the Pacific. Stilwell believed that the Japanese could be defeated only by a major land battle on the Asiatic mainland, spearheaded by Chinese manpower. But Chiang refused either to train or commit his troops to such a battle. Chennault, head of the U. S. 14th Air Force, and former chief of the volunteer "Flying Tigers" was certain he could turn the Japanese tide with his small air force of some 100 fighters and 50 bombers. And in Washington, the President and Chiefs of Staff considered neither Chennault's fliers nor Stilwell's ground forces for more than diversionary efforts to tie up Japanese troops, shipping and industry; they were instead committed to invading Japan through the Nimitz-MacArthur pincers in the Pacific islands.

With all these problems, and after a year and a half of stalemate broken only by the intermittent operations of the almost legendary Brigadier Orde Wingate and his Chindits behind Japanese lines, the Allies launched an offensive in Burma. Stilwell, with two American-trained Chinese divisions and Merrill's "Marauders," an American force designed on Chindit lines for irregular warfare, began to clear northern Burma with help from Chinese armies advancing west from Yunnan.

On the central front, Lt.-General William Slim's British-Indian 14th Army was to strike from Assam across the Kohima-Imphal plain to Mandalay, liberating central Burma, and then down the Irrawaddy River to Rangoon, thus clearing the Japanese from southern Burma. A third campaign under Lt.-General A. P.

Christison would move Indian and West-African divisions along the Bay of Bengal coast down the Arakan peninsula to Akyab.

After 18 months of bitter fighting, with more dead of hunger, disease and wounds than killed in combat, all three drives succeeded. A major defeat was inflicted on the Japanese on the Kohima-Imphal plain in July 1944, the Burma Road was reopened in January 1945, too late to do much good in the war. In May Rangoon fell to the combined assault of Slim's armies and airborne-amphibious troops. Burma was reconquered.

The campaign had been a disaster to the Japanese; with the Philippines, it was their largest land defeat in the entire war. They suffered more than 300,000 casualties, about 100,000 of these dead. The Allies also suffered severely, both from the Japanese and the disease-ridden Burmese jungles.

Events did ultimately show some of the differing ideas and leaders among the Allies to be correct. Though the American Air Transport Command, in a brilliant operation, flew supplies into China from northeast India over the 23,000-foot Himalaya Mountains, and American engineers and Chinese laborers performed prodigies in building the new Ledo Road to connect the old Burma Road, Churchill's estimate of Chiang's fighting capacity proved substantially correct. A spring 1944 Japanese ground offensive in South China took Chennault's airfields, and proved the now recalled Stilwell was right on that score: that the moment Chennault's planes really hurt the Japanese, they would simply take his bases. And Nimitz and MacArthur's successes were to prove Stilwell wrong about the necessity of defeating Japan on the Asiatic mainland with Chinese armies.

Nowhere was fighting fiercer than on the black volcanic sands of Iwo Ji

Iwo Jima: Hell's Acre

After Doolittle's fliers bombed Tokyo on April 18, 1942, Japan's home islands were not attacked for more than two years. Then, in July 1944, B-29's hit the Yawata steel works on northern Kyushu from bases in southwestern China, but not until the Superfortresses began to fly from the Marianas in November 1944 were the heavy industrial areas in Honshu within range nor could the home islands be subjected to large-scale, continuing bombardment. Even the Marianas were more than 1300 miles from Tokyo, a round trip just short of and sometimes longer than 3000 miles and 16 hours of flying time. Such a long flight unprotected by fighters meant reduced effectiveness and increased casualties, heavier gasoline loads and lightening the B-29's 10-ton bomb load capacity to 3 tons to make room for the extra fuel. To complicate matters, the Japanese were using Iwo Jima in the Bonin Islands, halfway between Saipan and Tokyo, as an advanced radar and fighter interceptor base to warn Tokyo of B-29 raids and to shoot the big Superforts down going to and coming from the home islands. The Japanese were also using Iwo to stage bombers in from Japan proper to raid the Superfort bases in the Marianas. With Iwo in American hands, not only could Japanese early warning and interception be forestalled, but the island's airfields could provide a base for P-51 Mustangs to give fighter escort to the B-29's, and Iwo could also serve as a staging, refueling, and rescue station for the big bombers coming from and going to Japan. As a result, the Navy and Marine Corps were assigned the task of taking Iwo.

While MacArthur in the Philippines and Mountbatten, Slim, and Sultan in Burma were giving the Japanese

175

armies their greatest land trouncings, Iwo Jima was treated to seven months of aerial and naval bombardment. For the 74 days immediately preceding the February 19, 1945, landing date, Iwo was bombed every day, and Formosa, Okinawa, and the Japanese home islands were subjected to neutralizing heavy strikes from carrier and land planes. In the last three days before D-Day, Admiral Spruance's Fifth Fleet smashed at the 8 square miles of Iwo with everything it had.

The Japanese too realized the importance of Iwo and on it had 23,000 first-class Japanese troops under Lieutenant General Tadamichi Kuribayashi entrenched in the most heavily fortified positions the Marines had yet encountered. The island was a maze of reinforced concrete pillboxes, bunkers, and blockhouses, beautifully camouflaged and connected by a labyrinth of underground tunnels and corridors. Guns were emplaced behind 4 to 6 feet of steel-reinforced concrete so that nothing short of a direct hit from a heavy-caliber naval gun could knock them out. Kuribayashi's tactics were to combine resistance on the beaches with defense in depth, so that major defense positions were concentrated at two strategic locations: the southern tip of Iwo, on and around the 554-foot extinct volcano, Mount Suribachi, from whose rim Japanese observers could spot any move on the island and from which Japanese guns were zeroed in on the only two possible landing beaches and their offshore waters; and at the widest part of the island around Motoyama Village north of Iwo's center. Guns of every caliber had been set up for interlocking fields of fire to cover almost the entire area of the small island, all protected with extensive minefields. From the naked black volcanic ash beaches steep slopes led up to Iwo's central plateau, where the two Japanese

Marines flush Japanese soldiers out of their deep bunkers on Iwo Jima.

The Fifth Marines raise the flag on Suribachi in the war's great picture.

airfields were located and a third was being built, and made ascent difficult. In addition to the rugged terrain of Mount Suribachi, whose code name was "Hotrocks," but whose Marine nickname "Mount Plasma" was perhaps more appropriate, the island's northern part was riddled with ravines and canyons, and honeycombed with fortified caves.

To take this island fortress, the Americans had assembled more than 800 ships, 1500 planes, and 3 reinforced Marine divisions of more than 60,000 men for the assault force. As they sailed for the Bonins the Marines jokingly sang, to the tune of "Argentina," a popular song of the day:

> **You know your life will begin**
> **The very moment you're in**
> **Iwo Jima ...**

It was a joke the survivors were to remember painfully.

On the morning of February 19, the 4th and 5th Marine Divisions stormed ashore on the southeast coast of Iwo along Futatsune Beach to meet withering Japanese fire. A little more than a day after the landings, the 5th Marine Division had isolated Mount Suribachi and sliced Iwo in two by knifing to the west coast. The 4th Marine Division, which had come ashore on the 5th's right flank, had struck inland and captured Motoyama Airfield No. 1. After three days of savage fighting, the southern third of the island was in American hands, "Mount Plasma" was conquered, and both divisions turned northward against the enemy. At 10:35 on the morning of February 23, a Marine patrol reached the top of Suribachi to hoist a small flag there. Later, when a larger Old Glory was raised, Associated Press photographer Joe Rosenthal took the most famous photograph of the Pacific war, a picture to be memorialized in bronze in a

179

statue, presented to the nation by the U. S. Marine Corps, which looks out over the Potomac from its site just north of Arlington National Cemetery. Dedicated in 1954, it is known officially as the Marine Corps Memorial.

The next day, February 24, the 3rd Marine Division, held in reserve, was ashore and put into the line across the island between the 5th on the left flank and the 4th on the right. Together they pushed forward slowly in a bloody operation in which all the immense firepower of American naval and air strength could only play a minor role. The dug-in Japanese had to be rooted out by frontal assault by Marines using tanks, bazookas, flame throwers, demolition charges, grenades, BARs, rifles, and bayonets in a slogging yard-by-yard, pillbox-by-pillbox advance. Time and again positions won had to be retaken as the Japanese returned through their hidden underground tunnels to attack the Marine rear. Combat correspondents gave this graphic account:

White clouds from American smoke grenades made the scene seem unearthly. It blew like steam across the ridge's stone walls. Three American tanks lay 50 yards away, firing their 75s point-blank at a concrete pillbox perched near the ridge's summit. The Marines attacking the ridge crawled among the stones and sandy shellholes, peering through the smoke for enemy movements.

A flamethrowing team, guarded by two automatic riflemen, worked its way cautiously up to an already-blackened hole. The air was filled with the noise of exploding grenades and with the smell of cordite and dead bodies.

The smoke blew away from one section of the rocks. The exposed stones and caves looked like an ogre's face, showing broken black and brown teeth, ready

to snap at the Marines attacking it. From behind one of the "teeth"—a black hole in the wall—a Nambu machine gun chattered. A Marine rifleman, caught upright, scrambled toward the protection of a boulder. He stopped abruptly, reached for his throat and fell to his knees. The machine gun kept chattering. The Marine screamed and slowly dropped to his full length.

It was ironic that at the time this ridge of death was almost a mile behind our front lines. Elements of the 9th and 21st Marines had first seized it several days before and, thinking it secured, had gone on. . . .

None of us suspected that there were still Japs in the desertlike area. The ridge had had its day already, and we assumed that its story was over. The Marines who had originally taken it on D plus 16 had clambered across it, first knocking out its gun positions with mortars, bazookas and tank fire, in the usual way, and then poking into every hole for surviving enemy. Some of the holes needed treatment with hand grenades and flamethrowers, while others were sealed with demolitions. But there had been little trouble, and soon the ridge had become quiet. The lines had gone on. Platoons had moved ahead, fighting through the lost world of the sulphur area, up to the third airfield. Support elements had followed, pausing near the ridge, then flowing on toward the northern end of the island. Finally an aid station had arrived and set up among the tumbled boulders. And that was when the fireworks, which we were now witnessing, had begun. . . .

A heavy Jap machine gun had suddenly rattled from the side of the ridge, just as a man carrying a crate of ammunition was passing by. He dropped his load of mortar shells, looked startled, and crumpled in a heap in the sand. A group of Marines, idling across the open space, hit the dirt and wriggled behind rocks. Two automatic riflemen, attached to a rifle company in reserve, peeked over the lip of the shellhole in which they had been resting. They tried to see where the bullets were coming from. They spotted an opening in the rocks and fired at it. The Jap machine gun ceased rattling. The two Marines cautiously clambered out of the shellhole and crawled toward the ridge. Other Marines, sensing a fight, waved to each other and began to close in. They covered each other with carbines and rifles and edged slowly toward the rocky hole.

A blaze of enemy small-arms fire came from at least five different parts of the ridge. Three Marines toppled over and the others dived for cover. The bullets whistled past the men in the aid station . . . .

When the tanks arrived, the Marines had started the step-by-step of again cleaning out the ridge. The dangerous and tedious work that had originally been done on D plus 16 by the front-line troops had to be repeated. The Marines threw smoke bombs and phosphorous grenades against the rocks and moved in with bazookas and automatic weapons. When the smoke drifted away, they had to shoot fast, or a Jap would catch them from one of the many holes. The tanks hurled their 75's at every position their gunners could locate. Engineers tried to fling dynamite charges into the caves.

Despite their preponderance of weapons, the Marines found that there were too many holes. . . .

Finally flamethrowers were called. They threw long jets of flaming liquid into the holes and along the curving walls of the tunnels. The roaring flames did the trick. The Marines heard the Japs howling. A few rushed out of the caves on fire. The Marines shot them or knocked them down and beat out the flame and took them prisoners. When the Marines began to hear muffled explosions inside the caves, they guessed that some of the Japs were blowing themselves up with hand grenades.

The scene became wild and terrible. More Japs rushed screaming from the caves. They tumbled over the rocks, their clothes and bodies burning fiercely. Soon the flamethrowers paused. A Marine lifted himself cautiously into view. There were no shots from the caves. . . .

The Japanese neither surrendered nor tried to escape from the island. Instead, they fought on savagely until March 16, when they were slowly pushed into the northwest part of Iwo Jima and annihilated on Kitano Point. Though Iwo was declared secure on that date, the operation was not concluded until March 26, and mopping up continued for nearly two months more. Iwo Jima had been a grueling, bloody battle, more costly than even Tarawa and Peleliu. Over 22,300 Japanese were killed or sealed up in caves, and perhaps a 1000 prisoners taken. But one of every three Marines in the fight was a casualty, with almost 20,000 Marine wounded and almost 6000 dead. In addition, Japanese kamikaze pilots had damaged the aircraft carrier Saratoga, sent the escort carrier Bismarck Sea to the bottom, and inflicted minor damages on several other naval vessels. In the process, they killed and wounded just short of 2800 sailors. Marine Corps General "Howlin' Mad" Smith said Iwo Jima was the toughest fighting the Marine Corps had met in its 168-year history, and Admiral Nimitz paid tribute to the Marines' victory, saying, "Among Americans who served on Iwo Island, uncommon valor was a common virtue."

Okinawa

Even while Iwo Jima was still being mopped up and MacArthur was liberating the Philippines, American forces leapfrogged 760 miles west of Iwo to the key island of the Ryukyu archipelago, 67-mile-long Okinawa. Strategically Okinawa was located so that bases there would permit American air and sea strikes on Kyushu, Formosa, and China, all some 350 miles away, and on shipping in Japanese coastal waters and the East China Sea, through which ran Japan's lifeline to its raw material resources in China and Southeast Asia. Okinawa was also an excellent springboard from which to invade Japan and could provide air cover for the final amphibious assault.

A week before invading Okinawa, the 77th Infantry Division, under command of Major General Andrew D.

A battleship pounds the beach at Okinawa while amphibious tractors head for

Bruce, seized the Kerama Retto, a small group of islands 15 miles west of Okinawa, to use for an advanced supply depot and seaplane base, and also for a fleet anchorage to repair, service, and replenish ships. Another small island between Kerama Retto and Okinawa, Keise Shima, was taken the day before the landing, and heavy artillery emplaced there to fire on southern Okinawa, only 8 miles away.

In March, after Fifth Fleet strikes on Kyushu and Honshu, and while B-29 assaults from the Marianas on the Japanese home islands mounted, Okinawa was plastered by 10 days of air and sea preparatory bombardment. An armada of more than 1450 ships with more than 1500 carrier planes for air cover was joined by a strong British battle squadron of 26 ships, including 2 battleships, 4 heavy carriers, 5 cruisers, and more than 240 planes, to carry Army Lieutenant

shore. The beaches came easy, but Japanese fought desperately in the hills.

General Simon Bolivar Buckner's U. S. Tenth Army to Okinawa. The Tenth Army included the Marine III Amphibious Corps under Major General Roy Geiger and the Army XXIV Corps under Major General John R. Hodge, 7 divisions totaling more than 450,000 men. At 8:30 on the morning of April 1, 1945, both Easter Sunday and All Fools' Day, the 1st and 6th Marine Divisions and the 7th and 96th Infantry Divisions landed abreast on the southwest coast of Okinawa on the Hagushi beaches. To their surprise they met no obstacles, and very little other opposition. The Marines quickly overran Yontan airfield and wheeled north, while the Army seized Kadena airfield and pivoted south. Both Japanese planes and installations were taken virtually intact.

If the landings looked so easy it was because the Japanese battle plan called for little resistance on the beaches or on most of the island. Lieutenant General Mitsuru Ushijima, commander at Okinawa, had pulled the bulk of his 100,000-man garrison into a powerful line of fortifications on the southern part of the island.

The strategy relied on a tactic improvised and briefly used in the Philippines, at Leyte and Lingayen Gulfs, and at Iwo Jima, but had been held in reserve for all-out use in case of just such a threat to Japan as invasion of Okinawa posed. To make up for critical losses in ships, planes and pilots, the Japanese High Command was now to resort to suicide tactics to tilt the scales of battle in their favor. The tactic was a desperate measure, a modification of the already well-known banzai charge, but now more purposefully organized for sea and air attack. Having sunk 16 ships and damaged 87 in the Philippines, and having crippled the carrier Saratoga and sank the escort carrier

Bismarck Sea off Iwo Jima, the Japanese now hoped to use these suicide tactics as a coordinated part of their battle plan. Suicide boats and planes would destroy or disperse the American fleet off Okinawa leaving the ground forces stranded without supplies or air and naval support. Once the Tenth Army was thus isolated, Ushijima hoped to annihilate it.

In capturing the Kerama Retto, the Americans had luckily seized almost 400 Japanese suicide boats there and so frustrated Japanese plans to send them crashing into American landing craft and transports off the Okinawa beaches. But the more important aerial suicide squads were based on Kyushu and Formosa and harder to reach. They were the "Special Attack Corps" the Japanese called kamikaze, which means "Divine Wind," and refers to the typhoon which dispersed Kublai Khan's invasion fleet when, in 1281, the Mongol Emperor tried to invade Japan. The kamikaze had first been organized by Vice-Admiral Takijiro Onishi in the hope that this modern "Divine Wind" would once again drive away the enemy fleets menacing the Japanese homeland.

Kamikaze weapons were obsolete stripped-down fighter planes jammed with explosives, or the Oka (cherry blossom), which Americans dubbed Baka (stupid), a piloted, rocket-propelled bomb with a 1-ton explosive warhead and a 600 mph speed, carried to its target slung beneath a bomber. Suicide pilots simply dove both into American ships, with first priority for carriers, to blow them up. The tactics were equally simple: either a coordinated series of mass attacks in waves—the so-called kikusui or "floating chrysanthemums," or small group and individual attacks, with kamikazes generally guided to the target and protected by a regular fighter-plane escort.

187

Dug deep into the caves of the Okinawa hills, the Japanese had to be forced

out with satchel charges and flamethrowers. The casualties were heavy.

A Japanese fighting to the end is burned to death by the flamethrowers.

On April 6, the Japanese threw 699 planes, 355 of them kamikazes, against the U. S. Fleet off Okinawa in the opening blow of a Japanese campaign of purposeful self-destruction which was to inflict tremendous damage and heavy casualties on the Americans. Even as American fighter pilots and anti-aircraft gunners fought to shoot them out of the sky, they wondered what manner of men these kamikaze were. Yasuo Kuwahara, one of the kamikaze pilots, tells what they were like:

Around the shaved skull of each Kamikaze was bound a small flag, the crimson rising sun over his forehead. These departures were never conducted in a perfunctory manner. There was much ceremony, much show, toasts and valiant speeches—most of which I had already learned by rote. . . .

Yes, the same words, the words I had heard so often on this runway during the past weeks—the voice droning nasally for several minutes, and then the conclusion: 'And so, valiant comrades, smile as you go. . . . There is a place prepared for you in the esteemed presence of your ancestors . . . guardian warriors . . . samurai of the skies. . . .'

At last it was time to sing the battle song:
"The Airman's color is the color of the cherry blossom,
Look, the cherry blossoms fall on the hills of Yoshino.
If we are born proud sons of the Yamato race,
Let us die fighting in the skies."

Then the final toast. The sake glasses were raised, the cry surged: "Tennoheika Banzai!" [Long live the Emperor]. The kamikaze were saying "Sayonara" now, laughing and joking as they climbed into their obsolete planes. . . . The old planes didn't matter, though. It

191

was a one-way trip . . . just then I could think of only one man.

There he was with Nakamura, walking toward me. He didn't look real. That was right; the spirit had left already. His body would mechanically fulfill the duty. What a strange smile carved on that waxen face. "Tell him! Tell him you'll cover him all the way that you'll die with him. But no, he doesn't want it, and something, something strangles all words. Your time will come soon enough, Kuwahara. . . ."

The lead slab in my chest was heavy now, weighing me down, crushing the words. "Tatsuno . . . I. . . ." Our hands met in an icy clasp. Nakamura stood by, looking down. . . .

"Remember . . ." the words came, "how we always wanted to fly together?" I looked into his eyes and bowed my head.

"I will follow you soon," I whispered.

Then he gave me something. "Here," he said, "take care of this for me. It's not much to send, but take care of it."

Quickly I looked away. Tatsuno had just given me his little finger. Our doomed men always left something of themselves behind, a lock of hair, fingernails, an entire finger—for cremation. The ashes were sent home to repose in the family shrine. There, in a special alcove, the ashes would reside with the pictures of ancestors. Once yearly, a priest would enter that room to pray. . . .

Our kamikaze were traveling in wedges of three— lethal arrows slicing toward the American ships . . . we looked ahead, Okinawa! . . . Far off, I saw the swaths of American ships . . . in the center of that task force was our quarry, four carriers, guarded by battleships and a perimeter of destroyers. . . .

The lead kamikaze dives, dropping vertically into a barbed-wire entanglement of flak. He'll never make the carriers; that seems obvious. Instead, he's heading for a cruiser near the fringe. For a moment it looks as if he'll make it. But no—he's hit, and it's all over. His plane is a red flare, fading, dropping from sight.

Everything is a blur now—a mixture of sound and color. Two more of them go the same way, exploding in mid-air. A fourth is luckier. He screams unscathed through the barrage, leveling inside the flak umbrella near the water. A hit! He's struck a destroyer right at the water line. A bellowing explosion, then another and another. It's good! It's good! The ship is in its death throes....

Tatsuno is alone now, still unhit, making a perfect run, better than they ever taught us in school. Tatsuno! Tatsuno! Fire spouts from his tail section, but he keeps going. The orange fingers reach out. His plane is a moving sheet of flame, but they can't stop him. Tatsuno! A tanker looms, ploughing the leaden liquid. They're closing! A hit! An enormous explosion rocks the atmosphere. For a curious instant embers seem to roll and dance. Now a staccato series of smaller bursts and one mighty blast, shaking the sea like a blanket. The tanker is going down. Gone. No trace but the widening shroud of oil.

That was my friend.

The kamikaze were all gone now, so far as I could tell. We had sunk a destroyer and a tanker, wounded a cruiser and (though I didn't learn it till later) severely damaged a battleship.

The Japanese had a desperate but effective weapon in their suicide squadrons. From the landings at Leyte Gulf to the end of the battle for Okinawa, kamikazes sank or damaged 475 ships. The destroyers on the picket line strung out to warn of the approach of "cherry blossoms" or "floating chrysanthemums" took the worst beating, but no ship was immune. Although the kamikazes sank nothing larger than an escort carrier, they damaged 12 carriers, 15 battleships, and 16 light and escort carriers. In the Okinawa battle alone, 1900 individual suicide attacks and 10 whole-sale assaults, in addition to ordinary dive-bombing and torpedo-bombing, resulted in 30 U. S. ships sunk, 368 damaged, and 9700 casualties in the fleet. Of every 7 naval casualties in World War II, one was suffered off Okinawa.

On the same day, April 5, that the "floating chry-santhemums" were ordered into battle, Admiral Soemu Toyoda, commander of the Japanese Combined Fleet, sent Vice-Admiral Seiichi Ito out of Tokuyama Bay with

At Okinawa, the Kamikazes almost turned the tide of battle. Even when hit o.

a 10-ship squadron that included the superbattleship Yamato, the light cruiser Yahagi, and 8 destroyers on what was essentially another suicide sortie; the squadron had only enough fuel to reach the Okinawa beaches, but not enough to return to Japan and it was dispatched without air cover. At dawn on April 8, Ito was to descend on the Hagushi beaches and his guns were to smash the landings. But the flotilla was sighted coming out of the Bungo Strait between Kyushu and Shikoku by American submarines which reported it to Admiral Spruance, who then had it tailed by spotter planes. On April 7 Admiral Mitscher threw 280 fighters, dive-bombers and torpedo-bombers at Ito's force and caught it southwest of Kyushu where in one afternoon he sank the Yamato, the Yahagi, and four destroyers.

In the meantime, ashore, four-fifths of Okinawa had been cleared by April 20, except for mopping up,

the way in, the suicide fliers were often able to crash into US targets.

after the Marines had smashed the Japanese on Motobu Peninsula in fierce mountain fighting. On April 16, the 77th Infantry Division, rested from its seizure of the Kerama Retto, landed on Ie Shima, the small island west of Okinawa where the Japanese had three airstrips. They took it in five days of bitter combat.

There, too, on April 18, after surviving so many brushes with death, Ernie Pyle died. Pyle, one of the soldiers' favorite newsmen, had tried to give Americans back home the soldier's-eye view of the fighting by living as much like the fighting men as he could. And he died like a fighting man, up front, killed by a Japanese machine-gun burst.

In the south, the Americans now hit Ushijima's main line of defense; three deep, the lines stretched across a three-mile-wide neck of the island, based on Naha on the west coast, Shuri in the center, and Yonabaru on the east coast. All exploited critical terrain features of that rugged country—Kakazu Ridge, Sugar Loaf Hill, and Conical Hill—into which the Japanese had dug a formidable combination of fortified positions. From these the Japanese drenched the Americans with the most accurate and heavy massed artillery fire they had yet used. From April 19 on, soldiers and Marines in infantry-tank assault teams hurled themselves forward and were beaten back with heavy casualties, viciously counterattacked by the Japanese, and bogged down in a sea of mud created by a week of torrential rains. Marine Sergeant Murray Lewis describes the combat infantryman's plight:

Okinawa's rainy season arrived while the fighting was still going on. Here is what it was like in one foxhole on the slope of a hill, perhaps seven feet long and three feet wide.

In it lay a Marine who at first could not be dis-

tinguished from the jellied terrain around him. He wore no poncho because it would have impeded him if he had had to advance.

He was soaked to the skin and the soft mud had been packed into clay over his face and clothing. He had spent a sleepless night, drenched in the water pouring steadily from the gray skies, and his eyes were red-rimmed with weariness. All through the night the Japs had kept up an intermittent artillery and mortar barrage into the area and for each dragging minute of that night he had heard the soft crunch of the deadly shells hitting the earth around him.

Occasionally there was a cry of pain, but he was too full of his own woes to think too much of it. Perhaps a hospital corpsman could break through in the morning to aid the wounded. Perhaps he couldn't.

The Marine had had a breakfast of sorts, only because he felt he should eat something. His rations were slimy, crusted with soft mud which had seeped into the small can of pork and egg yolks, eaten cold because a fire was impossible. Afterward he pulled a cigarette from the cache in his helmet, but that had been soaked, too.

He had his rifle under his body, although he knew he could never hope to keep it really dry. But he had it ready. His eyes stared ahead probing the blackness for a possible counterattack and wishing it would happen, yet hoping it wouldn't. In this war of opposing lines usually no more than fifty yards apart, the fighting went on regardless of weather conditions. The artillery duel was just as intense as it was two days ago, though the rain muffled the boom of the heavy guns into a shapeless roar.

"Don't let me be wounded in this mud," he prayed. "Don't let me get hit bad."

While B-29s turned Japanese cities into charred ruins, American submarines

After prolonged and bloody fighting, Buckner's soldiers and Marines broke through the Japanese positions. Naha fell on May 27, Shuri a few days later, and by June 22, Ushijima and his chief of staff, Lieutenant General Isamo Cho, had committed hara-kari and organized resistance on Okinawa was over. General Buckner had not lived to see the final victory; on June 18, at a forward observation post, the Tenth Army commander was killed by Japanese shellfire while observing a Marine infantry and armor attack

The last major amphibious assault of the Pacific war, Okinawa was one of the toughest and longest. In its grueling three months both sides had suffered severe losses. Almost 110,000 Japanese troops were killed, but for the first time a large group surrendered. Some 7400 Japanese soldiers did go "into the bag," more than all the rest combined for the entire Pacific war, though more might have been saved had Ushijima accepted General Buckner's offer to capitulate when it was obvious that the Japanese position was hopeless. In the battle for Okinawa, the Japanese lost 7800 aircraft and more than 12,000 airmen, most of their heavy equipment on the island, and a good portion of the remaining vestiges of their once proud battle fleet. The Americans lost more than 760 planes, 36

...ut off essential imports and brought Japanese industry virtually to a halt.

ships sent to the bottom and 368 damaged, and in addition to the 9700 naval casualties, there were 7613 dead, 31,807 wounded, and another 26,000 noncombat casualties, altogether a very costly campaign. But Americans now stood on Japan's doorstep, ready to step on to the sacred soil of the homeland.

The End in the East

In spite of the truly crippling devastation wrought by the B-29s, a skillful combination of censorship and propaganda had kept the Japanese people convinced that they were winning the war. The ruling elite, however, knew better but was divided on the course to take. The militarist clique (the Gumbatsu), led by the generals, called for a fight to the finish with such slogans as "One Hundred Million People Die in Honor!" and "Better to Die Than Seek Ignominious Safety." With the vast bulk of their Army intact and never even committed to battle, the generals hoped that a desperate defense of the homeland with its 2,500,000-man Army and almost 10,000 planes, many of them kamikazes, might either defeat the impending invasion or inflict such staggering losses on the Americans that they would drop their demand for

199

American bombers — B-29s (above) — based on captured islands came in to blast what was left of Japanese industry.

"unconditional surrender" and be disposed to discuss a compromise peace. In that event, the generals thought they could not only save themselves, but negotiate better terms for the nation.

The great industrial interests (the Zaibatsu), led by the Emperor and the Jushin had been joined by Navy leaders, whose once proud fleet now had been shattered, in cautiously trying to end the war.

After Saipan, the Jushin and the Lord Keeper of the Privy Seal, Marquis Kido, had succeeded in forcing Tojo out of office, but the new cabinet under General Kuniaki Koiso, even with a Jushin deputy Premier, Admiral Mitsumasa Yonai, had not been able to work openly to end the war, and had continued its vigorous prosecution instead. On April 5, 1945, five days after the Okinawa landings, the Koiso cabinet collapsed and two days later 79-year-old Admiral Kantaro Suzuki became Premier, supported by Kido, the Jushin, and the Emperor. Suzuki could muster three "peace faction" votes in the inner cabinet, the Supreme War Council — Foreign Minister Shigenori Togo's, Navy Minister Admiral Mitsumasa Yonai's, and his own — but he was resolutely opposed by the War Minister and

the Army and Navy Chiefs Staff.

On the same day Koiso's cabinet fell, the USSR denounced its 1941 neutrality pact with Japan, taking the first step toward entering the Pacific war, as it had long promised the Allies, and which it had nailed down at Yalta. Another and more grievous blow came on May 6, when the Germans surrendered. Japan was now alone and at bay, and its rulers knew that soon all the great Allied strength would be turned from Germany on Japan.

In Washington, in the meantime, several American diplomats, notably Secretary of War Henry L. Stimson and acting Secretary of State and former Ambassador to Japan, Joseph Grew, urged President Truman to make a public statement guaranteeing that neither the Japanese nation or monarchy would be destroyed under the terms of "unconditional surrender." Such a proclamation, they believed, might bring peace without the bloodletting of an invasion. Truman, still new to the Presidency, hesitated. Strong pressure was exerted by various segments of the American public, and by China and Russia, to hold Hirohito responsible for the war and to try him as a war criminal. Many American leaders also believed such a proclamation would seem to be a confession of American weakness, an unwillingness to endure such sacrifices as the last-ditch Japanese defenses of Okinawa had imposed, and would only prolong the war. As a result, no such statement was made.

Instead, operations were launched to knock out Japan's remaining air and naval power and so soften it up for the impending invasion. Halsey's Third Fleet cruised along the Japanese east coast virtually unopposed, shelling ports, ships, factories, and other installations. Mitscher's carrier planes sank coastal shipping, smashed air fields and airplanes, and in a series of lethal strikes on the naval bases at Kure and Yokosuka sank or damaged and put out of action almost all the remaining ships of Japan's fleet, including 8 battleships and aircraft carriers. General Curtis LeMay's Superforts continued to reduce Japan's great cities to rubble, and the Allies were now to introduce a new and fearful weapon.

In August 1939, physicist Albert Einstein had written to President Roosevelt advising him that nuclear fission might produce a bomb more devastating than any weapon ever before devised. In a secret combined effort with Canada and Great Britain, Roosevelt had authorized a vast research and production effort to make such a bomb, and because secrecy was absolutely necessary, had done so without Congressional consent. After five years of work by 125,000 people in the United States, and expenditure of more than $2,000,000,000, the bomb was now a reality. On July 17, while Truman was at the Potsdam Conference, he received a brief message—"Babies satisfactorily born"—informing him that the first atomic test explosion had been set off successfully at Alamogordo in the New Mexico desert. Truman, with Churchill's concurrence, approved its use against Japan to bring the war to a swift end and to avoid the enormous casualties anticipated in an invasion.

On July 26, 1945, President Truman issued a "Proclamation to the Japanese People," later known as the Potsdam Declaration, which called on Japan to surrender unconditionally or face prompt and utter destruction, but no specific mention was made of the atomic bomb. The Declaration was more than one remove from unconditional surrender. Under its terms, Japan was to be stripped of its conquests and its sovereignty reduced to the home islands. Japan's militarists would have to be tried and punished, and "Freedom of speech, of religion, and of thought, as well as respect for the fundamental human rights, shall be established." Japan's war industries would have to be liquidated, Japan would have to pay reparations, its armed forces would have to be totally disarmed, and it would have to endure Allied military occupation. If Japan capitulated promptly, however, its armies would be "permitted to return to their homes, with the opportunity of leading peaceful and productive lives," the Allied occupation would not be prolonged, and, the Allies promised, "We do not intend that the Japanese shall be enslaved as a race nor destroyed as a nation."

Though the Declaration met with some approval in the Japanese Supreme War Council and the Emperor accepted it "in principle," the Japanese decided to wait and see what Soviet mediation might produce. In a press conference on July 29, Premier Suzuki stated that he would ignore the Potsdam Declaration, and no further official response was forthcoming. The die was now cast; the atomic bomb would be used.

On August 3, President Truman issued the order to use the atomic bombs on any one of four targets— Hiroshima, Kokura, Niigata, or Nagasaki. The bombs had already been brought from San Francisco to Tinian where a special group of B-29s was to deliver them. On August 6, 1945, the first flight of three Superfortresses set out for Hiroshima. One of them,the Enola Gay, flown by Colonel Paul W. Tibbets, Jr., carried the bomb; two others went along as observers. The effect was so devastating that Colonel Tibbets said, "Saw city, destroyed same." A Japanese told Marcel Junod, Red Cross representative, of what the bomb did:

Suddenly a glaring whitish-pink light appeared in the sky accompanied by an unnatural tremor that was followed almost immediately by a wave of suffocating heat and a wind that swept away everything in its path.

Within a few seconds the thousands of people in the streets and the gardens in the center of the town were scorched by a wave of searing heat. Many were killed instantly, others lay writhing on the ground, screaming in agony from the intolerable pain of their burns. Everything standing upright in the way of the blast, walls, houses, factories, and other buildings, was annihilated: and the debris spun round in a whirlwind and was carried up into the sky. Trams were picked up and tossed aside as though they had neither weight nor solidity. Trains were flung off the rails as though they were toys. Horses, dogs, and cattle suffered the same fate as human beings. Every living thing was petrified in an attitude of indescribable suffering. Even the vegetation did not escape. Trees went up in flames, the rice plants lost their greenness, the grass burned on the ground like dry straw.

Beyond the zone of utter death in which nothing remained alive, houses collapsed in a whirl of beams, bricks, and girders. Up to about three miles from the center of the explosion, lightly built houses were flattened as though they had been built of cardboard. Those who were inside were either killed or wounded. Those who managed to extricate themselves by some miracle found themselves surrounded by a ring of fire. And the few who succeeded in making their way to safety, generally died twenty or thirty days later from the delayed effects of the deadly gamma rays. . . .

By evening the fire began to die down and then it went out. There was nothing left to burn. Hiroshima had ceased to exist.

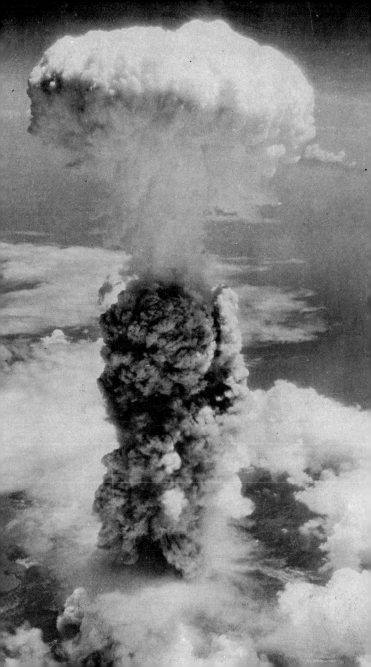

Two days after Hiroshima, while Japanese Ambassador to Moscow Naotake Sato continued to urge Russian mediation with the Allies, he was handed a declaration of war. Marshal Aleksandr Vasilevski sent the Red Army plunging into Manchuria from three directions. Though the Kwantung Army still had almost 700,000 troops behind powerful fortifications, it had long been weakened by successive reinforcements to the islands and homeland, and was unable to put up effective resistance. The Red Army overran Manchuria and the southern half of Sakhalin.

While the Japanese Supreme War Council continued to haggle over the Potsdam terms, the second plutonium atomic bomb was exploded over Nagasaki at 11:01 A.M. on August 9. Because of the way the terrain lay, its effect was not as annihilating as the one over Hiroshima, but 73,884 were killed, and 60,000 injured.

On August 14, the Supreme War Council decided to capitulate and prepared a recording of the Imperial rescript announcing the surrender. But the military fanatics were by no means ready to acquiesce. Once they got wind of the plan, they plunged into violent action. That night, officers of the War Ministry and General Staff attempted a coup d'état. Quick action by officers and troops loyal to the Emperor quelled the mutiny, and on the next day, August 15, the Japanese people for the first time heard the voice of their Emperor. He told them, in court Japanese that many had to have translated, and without mentioning the word "surrender," that the war was over.

Opposition to the surrender was still not over. There was a wave of riots, demonstrations, and suicides, especially among high-ranking Army and Navy officers.

Only the direct intervention of the Emperor, ordering people and fighting men alike to "suffer the insufferable and bear the unbearable" prevented a full-scale revolt.

At 9:04 A.M., on Sunday, September 2, 1945, three years, eight months, and one week after Pearl Harbor, six years and one day since Hitler's Wehrmacht had launched its blitzkrieg on Poland, and 14 years after the Kwantung Army had invaded Manchuria, the holocaust was ended on the decks of the battleship Missouri anchored in Tokyo Bay. There, General Douglas MacArthur signed the formal instrument of surrender for the Allies and Foreign Minister Mamoru Shigemitsu and Chief of Staff Yoshijiro Umezu signed for the Japanese, while military and naval leaders from America, Britain, Russia, and China were witness. All over the world, church bells tolled, sirens and whistles shrieked, and the people rejoiced. The monstrous anger of the guns was stilled; the war was over.

The peace had been earned at so appalling a cost that it could never accurately be counted. Even the estimates were so huge they were literally beyond the individual's capacity to feel them in human terms. How could one really understand that 17,000,000 troops had been killed and 18,000,000 civilians annihilated; that a total of some 35,000,000 human beings no longer walked the earth? How could the imagination encompass a deliberate German program of genocide which had exterminated 6,000,000 Jews, 6,000,000 Poles, and another 6,000,000 Russians, not to speak of hundreds of thousands of others murdered, beheaded, tortured, beaten, starved, and humiliated by Germans and Japanese alike?

When the economic costs were reckoned as more than $1,100,000,000,000 for direct military costs and another $2,100,000,000,000 in property damages, weren't those numbers so astronomical as to be

beyond real appreciation? And who could truly measure the cities left a welter of ruins and debris, the scorched earth and flooded fields, the ruined factories and mines, the decimated herds and flocks?

Everywhere, famine, hunger, and disease stalked Europe and Asia; millions of uprooted, homeless, and displaced people could find neither a place to rest nor shelter, nor useful work for their hands to do and for their minds to be occupied with; and millions more of the wounded and permanently disabled struggled to restore some semblance of normalcy to their lives. Millions of the fighting men who returned home apparently whole, more fortunate than the rest who would never come home again, were themselves "walking wounded," ill-at-ease and out of place.

At best, too, it was an uneasy peace. If the old world of tyranny, inequity, and injustice was not yet dead, neither did the new world being born, its throes violent and brutal, promise greater improvement. If the Nazi-Fascist-Japanese Axis had been broken and defeated, a new totalitarianism menaced the world. If the old imperialism was dead, a new imperialism, even more oppressive and exploiting, had been born. If the old nationalisms had been somewhat tempered and abated, new and fanatic nationalisms were soon to explode on the world. In Eastern Europe, the Soviet Union now controlled a dozen new countries and 100,000,000 people were soon to be yoked to Communism. On the Asiatic mainland, China was soon to be in Communist hands. Not only was the peace quickly turned into a "cold war," but in June 1950, only five years after the end of hostilities aboard the Missouri, a hot war had broken out in Korea.

All would have done well to remember the words Franklin Roosevelt had spoken on June 14, 1942:

Japanese representatives (above) board the battleship Missouri to surrender. While British, French, Chinese and Russian delegates look on and General Jonathan Wainright, a prisoner since the fall of Bataan, stands behind his old commander, General Douglas MacArthur signs the surrender document. The world's most devastating war has come to its end.

...Our earth is but a small star in the great universe. Yet of it we can make, if we choose, a planet unvexed by war, untroubled by hunger or fear, undivided by senseless distinctions of race, color or theory. Grant us that courage and foreseeing to begin this task today that our children and our children's children may be proud of the name of Man....

credits

THE WORDS

16-18
Ryan, Cornelius; from The Longest Day. Simon and Schuster, Inc., © 1959 by Cornelius Ryan. Reprinted by permission of the publisher and Victor Galloncz, London.
23-28
Pyle, Ernie; from Brave Men. Holt, Rinehart & Winston, Inc., © 1943, 1944 by Scripps-Howard Newspaper Alliance, © 1944 by Holt, Rinehart & Winston, Inc. Reprinted by permission of the publisher.
66-71
Marshall, S. L. A.; from Bastogne. Infantry Journal Press, 1946. Reprinted by permission of the Association of the United States Army.
110-117
Thompson, R. W.; from Men Under Fire. © 1945 by R. W. Thompson and The Sunday Times, London. Dispatch, ex R. W. Thompson to The Sunday Times, Belsen, Thursday, 19 April, 1945.
146-147
Sherrod, Robert; from On to Westward. Duell, Sloan & Pearce, Inc., © 1945 by Robert Sherrod. Reprinted by permission of the publisher, an affiliate of Meredith Press.
150-152
Josephy, Alvin M.; from The Long and the Short and the Tall. © 1946 by Alfred A. Knopf, Inc. Reprinted by permission of the publisher and author.
180-183
Marine Combat Correspondents; from US Marines on Iwo Jima. © 1945 by Dial Press and the Infantry Journal, Inc. Reprinted by permission of the publishers.
191-193
Kuwahara, Yasuo and Gordon T. Allred; from Kamikaze. Ballantine Books, Inc., © 1957 by Gordon T. Allred. Reprinted by permission of the publisher.
196-197
US Marine Corps Combat Correspondents (extract by Murray Lewis); from Semper Fidelis. Reprinted by permission of the Leatherneck Association and William Sloane Associates.
204-206
Junod, Marcel; from Warrior Without Weapons. The Macmillan Co., © 1951 by Marcel Junod. Reprinted by permission of the publisher and Jonathan Cape Ltd.

HE PHOTOGRAPHS

215